MEXICO AND THE CARIBBEAN

LEWIS HANKE

Professor of Latin American History
Columbia University

AN ANVIL ORIGINAL

under the general editorship of

LOUIS L. SNYDER

Modern Latin America: Continent in Ferment.
Volume I

D. VAN NOSTRAND COMPANY, INC.

PRINCETON, NEW JERSEY

TORONTO   LONDON

NEW YORK

To the memory of

MIRON BURGIN

who advised historians to
be concerned with the present

D. VAN NOSTRAND COMPANY, INC.
120 Alexander St., Princeton, New Jersey (*Principal office*); 24 West 40 St., New York, N.Y.
D. VAN NOSTRAND COMPANY (Canada), LTD.
25 Hollinger Rd., Toronto 16, Canada
D. VAN NOSTRAND COMPANY, LTD.
358, Kensington High Street, London, W.14, England

PREFACE

Not only is Latin America a continent in ferment, but the people and policy makers of the United States are in a ferment about Latin America. This volume is designed to set forth the nature of the fundamental problems today in Mexico, Central America, the Caribbean islands, Colombia, and Venezuela. A companion volume in this series treats of the other countries of Spanish America and Brazil. Both volumes have been prepared for students taking courses on international affairs, U.S. diplomatic history, and modern Latin America, and also for the growing number of concerned and thoughtful citizens in the United States and in the hemisphere generally who are pondering the fate of their countries.

The vast and variegated region arbitrarily called "Latin America"—a label no truer than the term "Yankee" applied indiscriminately to all U.S. citizens whether from Alabama, Maine, or Texas—cannot be easily described as a unit or confidently summed up. Any attempt to tell all in a brief work such as this would inevitably fail; thus this volume is neither a formal history nor an encyclopedic manual. The objective has been to acquaint the reader with sufficient information and variety of viewpoints to enable him to approach an understanding of Latin America as its countries enter another revolutionary period in their spectacular lives.

While I have leaned heavily on the contributions of my colleagues in many lands, the text necessarily indicates my own selection of problems to be considered and reflects my personal views. The documents illustrate the sharply divergent convictions held inside and outside of Latin America. This book will fail in its purpose if the readers do not see that under these interpretations made both by Latin Americans and by students of Latin America lies a common concern for sound democratic development in this great area of the world. The list of other readings includes additional publications which exist in great quantity and stimulating variety. I hope that the material in both text and documents will be only the starting point for further study in which other facts and viewpoints will be brought to bear.

The picture that emerges in this book is a sober and often a somber one, and always complex and confusing. I have attempted to paint it with historical perspective, realism, and sympathy; I hope the reader will remember that this rapid survey of basic social and economic problems must necessarily deal summarily with, or even omit, many important aspects of the achievements of Latin America. Difficulties and disturbing situations are to be found in all lands, including the United States; the encouraging fact about Latin America now is that her most farsighted leaders are confronting their reality and working for peaceful change.

Already significant advances have been made on many fronts. The position of Latin America today is so far superior to its condition in 1900, or even 1930, that one cannot doubt that further advances will be made by a continent with such resources of intelligence and vitality. Latin America is, indeed, in ferment, but it is a necessary ferment if the dreams of her peoples are to be fulfilled.

ACKNOWLEDGMENTS

I have received much help in the preparation of this volume from my wife and from Charles L. Eastlack, whose expert hand is also responsible for many of the translations. The Research Institute of the University of Texas made available to me Marvin Goldwert's assistance in collecting materials, and the excellent typing aid of Mrs. Lois Brubaker and Mrs. Iona Kay Stephenson. The patience of the editor of this series, Louis L. Snyder, and his encouragement as the work progressed were truly noteworthy.

The following friends and colleagues generously read portions of the text and documents and gave me the benefit of their comments and counsel: Orlando Fals-Borda, C. H. Haring, R. A. Humphreys, Thomas F. McGann, Richard M. Morse, E. V. Niemeyer, Jr., Stanley Robert Ross, Stanley J. Stein, and Bryce Wood; others were George A. Brubaker, Duvon Corbitt, Wendell Gordon, William Griffith, Simon G. Hanson, John P. Harrison, Fritz Hoffmann, Muna Lee, Edwin Lieuwen, Frank Knapp, Jr., Malcolm D. McLean, Robert G. Mead, Jr., David L. Miller, J. L. Mecham, Alfredo Navarrete, Eastin Nelson, Frederick B. Pike, Robert A. Potash, Henry Schmidt, Karl M. Schmitt, and Watt Stewart.

To all who have had a share in the completion of this work, I wish to express deep appreciation. The responsibility for the judgments expressed and for the nature of the book rests, of course, upon me alone.

Austin, Texas   LEWIS HANKE
October, 1959

TABLE OF CONTENTS

PART II—SELECTED READINGS

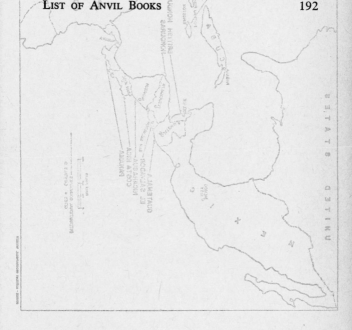

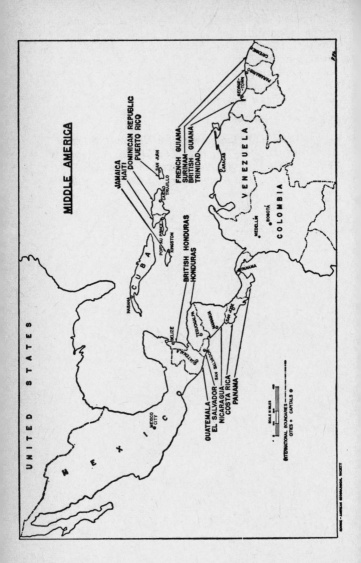

INTRODUCTION:
CONTINENT IN FERMENT

Latin America Enters the World Scene. The 20 republics south of the Rio Grande have come of age internationally in the twentieth century. In 1899 only Brazil and Mexico were deemed of sufficient importance to receive invitations to the first Hague Peace Conference. All the Latin American nations were invited to the second conference in 1907, and 18 attended. Henceforth Latin Americans were both seen and heard at international conference tables.

Their influence grew slowly, however. They played no large part in World War I, except as sources of raw materials. During the 1920's most Latin American nations joined the League of Nations, partly as a protection against the power of the United States, and at times played an active role in Geneva. During World War II Latin America gained greatly in prestige and strength. By 1945 she was ready to exert a more steady and significant pressure on world affairs than ever before. She participated vigorously in the establishment of the United Nations, supplied a considerable number of elected and appointed officers to the organization, and for the first ten years Latin America's 20 votes constituted a powerful bloc in the General Assembly. When 19 new members were admitted in 1957, numerical primacy passed to the Asian-African bloc and with it special power in the Assembly, although Latin America remains a force in the U.N. In such specialized agencies as UNESCO, Latin Americans and their projects have been vital from the beginning, and today one of its three principal activities

is the development of fundamental education in which
Mexico has played a prominent part.

Yet the leaders and peoples of this vast region are more
discontented than ever before, and they are distinctly unhappy with what they consider their unsatisfactory position in the world today. "Pan-Americanism has been tail-
ending," wrote the late Carlos Dávila, and he charged
that Latin America has had merely a vicarious sense of
weight in world affairs through the power of the United
States.

Disenchantment in the Good Neighborhood. Latin
Americans are dissatisfied above all with their position in
the Western Hemisphere, and with what they regard as
neglect by the United States since 1945. Although politically their position has greatly improved in the conduct
of the Organization of American States since the Charter
of 1948, they compare the $36 billion distributed to Eu-
rope in the period 1945-1957 through economic and
military aid with the approximately $3.5 billion sent to
Latin America and conclude that the Good Neighbor
Policy has ended. They are convinced that the worldwide concerns of the United States have permanently
diminished their relationship with us, and they fear that
the struggle between Soviet Russia and the United States
will drag them into unwanted controversies. They dislike
the seeming approval that the United States accords to
some dictators, and they attack military aid to their countries as aid to dictators against their own peoples. They
have been unsuccessful in obtaining price supports for
the export commodities on which their economies depend,
and desire more investment of U.S. Government capital.
They feel, too, that we underestimate their culture, know
little about their history, and ignore their aspirations.
Many of them fear, too, that the United States at times
is chiefly interested in the number of Communists in Latin
America, and our policy seems to them to revolve around
this subject in which they take relatively little interest.

Nor do Latin Americans share the hope that characterizes the emerging peoples of Africa and Asia. The
countries of Latin America won their political independence over a century ago and now have few utopian illu-
sions. They have seen great economic progress but no

comparable improvement in the lot of the masses who are still hungry, sick, and exploited. The enormous changes in their social and economic life have not been accompanied for the most part by corresponding developments in political institutions or political stability.

To aggravate the situation, Latin America's population grows at the explosive rate of 2.5 per cent annually, while the figure for the world as a whole is about 1.6 per cent. The present population of about 185 million is expected to reach 300 million by 1975 and 592 million by the year 2000, or almost twice the estimated population for the United States and Canada at that date. Given the present low standards in education and living conditions, thoughtful Latin Americans foresee continued economic insufficiency and social disturbance. They are beginning to search for assistance outside the hemisphere, specifically in Europe and even in Communist countries. In recent years the flow of European investments in Latin America expanded significantly, and West Germany now ranks second to the United States in capital invested in Brazil. French banks have transferred capital from Indochina and North Africa to Latin America. Latin Americans also are seeking new markets outside the hemisphere for their commodity exports.

The United States on its side is taking a new look at Latin America, particularly since the attacks on Vice-President Nixon in 1958 and the stoning of the U.S. Embassy in Bolivia in March, 1959. Have the money and technical assistance sent there accomplished what its recipients hoped and believed it would? Is the area always to have dictatorial governments and unstable economies? Will the governing elites never work out a program to educate the masses of their countrymen and incorporate them as responsible participants in the national life?

Beginning with Bolívar, a mystique developed in the countries of the Americas concerning their common destiny as New World nations. At Pan American conferences and elsewhere the oratory flowed copiously on this topic. One veteran U.S. specialist on inter-American affairs has now concluded that the Pan American movement—in the sense of a Western Hemisphere separated from Europe, whose countries were all joined together in a special relationship—entered into its final phase in 1940 and now is over, with the world divided into the Communist and non-Communist worlds.

Another veteran Latin Americanist considers this death announcement somewhat premature, but has become discouraged by studying the economic history of Latin America, especially the story of foreign investments and Point IV programs there. For many years a liberal-minded and sympathetic observer, this professor now maintains, in the mood of a disillusioned U.S. taxpayer, that Latin Americans have been on the whole rather ungrateful recipients of U.S. largesse, and that they are getting about all they deserve. He describes the Pan American Highway as a poor investment, the Rama Road in Nicaragua as a swindle, the rubber planting experiments in tropical America as a fiasco, and other well-meaning attempts to aid Latin America as unfortunate. He deplores U.S. aid to Bolivia, but holds out no hope for extricating ourselves from our predicament there. He sees great and almost insuperable difficulty in the way of any U.S. policy to favor popularly elected governments with economic aid while discriminating against dictatorships, and argues that no distinction should be made.

Another university specialist, with wide experience in Caribbean affairs, holds that U.S. public opinion gets unnecessarily excited about dictators and would have us pay no attention to the vagaries of the government in power because "political patterns for generations have followed certain trends in time and space in the Caribbean area as well as elsewhere in Latin America. Consequently, no one in the United States today should become disturbed by revolutions or dictators in the nations south of us. The people of these countries are simply engaged in practical politics. They think that our political methods are peculiar, just as we often think that their methods are impracticable. But they have developed workable governments as they developed their political habits. It is not for us to be alarmed or to become excited by their political practices. Their governments function as they want them to. They are satisfied with them. Who are we to criticize?"

A former Secretary of State has a different view from the academic experts. We cannot avoid taking positive action in Latin America, he holds, but feels that "a far greater effort is needed to arrive at mutual understanding and respect. But we must be careful not to act as the schoolmistress of the Western Hemisphere. We have a proper stake in how their governments behave toward us and affect our interests. We can properly object to infringements of them, or to conduct or to relations with our enemies or potential enemies likely to weaken the security of all of us. We can properly act to help them to participate in the life and to reap the benefits of a free world economic system. When we begin to take action as a government, to oppose suspensions of representative government and *habeas corpus,* and to berate those responsible, we are moving out of the area of proper conduct. Here I am preaching what I have learned the hard way. To express collective indignation may bring the glow of moral principles vindicated without effort; but it is usually futile and more often than not, harmful. . . ."

Another writer long concerned with U.S. public policy has warned against the delusion that democracy is the absence of dictators, that democracy can be attained by the revolutionary overthrow of dictators. He also warns against self-righteousness because "almost invariably, national self-righteousness is dominant in the breast of the interventionists or quasi-interventionists who advocate forcing the Latin Americans to live up to our concept of political democracy. It is outspoken among those who would have us turn our backs on the other American republics because they are unworthy of us." Our policy must be, he concludes, "for democracy rather than merely against dictators; it must be coöperative rather than self-righteous and denunciatory; it must be candid rather than conspirational." [1] Other U.S. observers of the Latin

[1] The three professors referred to are, respectively: Arthur P. Whitaker, *The Western Hemisphere Idea: Its Rise and Decline,* Ithaca, N.Y.: Cornell University Press, 1954, pp. 154, 176-177; J. Fred Rippy, *Globe and Hemisphere. Latin America's Place in the Postwar Foreign Relations of the United States,* Chicago: Henry Regnery, 1958, and his article "U.S. Aid to Latin America," *Journal of Inter-American Studies,* I (University of Florida, 1959), pp. 83-96; and A. Curtis Wilgus, *The Caribbean: Contemporary Trends,* Gainesville: University of Florida Press, 1953, pp. xxv-xxvi.

American scene are disquieted by the widespread assumption there that the United States is responsible for all the ills of Latin America, including the culture clash between the old and the new that is going on all over the region, and by the social and economic strains found there.

During World War II Latin America, except for Argentina, experienced a kind of honeymoon with the United States; this period is now definitely over, and both parties are in a mood of sober re-assessment. Latin American leaders are more determined and more articulate than ever before in presenting to the world the needs and aspirations of their continent in ferment. (*See Readings Nos. 1-14.*)

— 1 —

CENTRAL AMERICA

Sub-Continent in Crisis. The large land mass separating Mexico from South America has always been one of the least-known areas in the new world. Relatively few tourists go there despite its many attractions, and some diplomats are inclined to look upon appointment there as an assignment to Siberia. Only when one of its many volcanoes erupts, or when Communism is believed to be about to take over one of the republics, or when an archaeological expedition discovers some new ruin, does Central America make the news.

The 10 million people who live in this sub-continent

The two public officials cited are: (1) Dean Acheson, *Power and Diplomacy*, Cambridge: Harvard University Press, 1958, p. 180; (2) Y [Louis J. Halle], "On a Certain Impatience with Latin America," *Foreign Affairs*, XXVIII (New York, 1950), pp. 565-579. The quotations appear on pp. 577, 579.

have much in common, despite many dissimilarities. All six countries—Costa Rica, El Salvador, Guatemala, Honduras, Nicaragua, and Panama—formed a part of the vast Spanish Empire which lasted for almost four centuries. When independence came in 1821, except for Panama, the nations equally lacked political experience, a fact which helps to explain their nineteenth-century tribulations. With the coming of the present century, some parts of Latin America developed steadily, but Central America lagged behind, with the exception of Costa Rica.

Although there are some rugged mountains and high plateaus, much of the area is tropical and subject to severe, steady rain. In the lowlands some sections are deluged with 15 feet per year, and even the higher regions average 6 feet annually. Thus land communications remain an enormous problem. Although in only two—Honduras and Panama—do bananas constitute the principal export crop, all other countries have only one significant export—coffee—except Nicaragua where cotton is now dominant and Costa Rica where bananas share honors with coffee. Little manufacturing is done in the area and a middle class scarcely exists.

The population has a social complexion far from uniform. Costa's Rica's citizens are largely of European stock, while more than half of Guatemalans are Indians. Negroes are concentrated in the hot, coastal areas, but everywhere mulattoes, mestizos, and other racial combinations are to be found. Nearly 70 per cent of the population is rural, and in the rural areas the family group holds sway under a patriarchal system. A few hundred wealthy families in each country own most of the land and live in leisure and security. The vast majority suffer a life of drudgery, earning $200 or less per person annually.

Little attention or money has been devoted to education. The Catholic Church has been able to exert relatively slight influence. More than half of the people are illiterate and, despite dormant wealth, the republics of Central America exist in a state of poverty. Government intervention to develop national industries and control exchange has been a favorite occupation in recent years but has sometimes been ill-planned and inflationary. Economic productivity has increased but minutely, and the

wealthy tend to invest in real estate or in foreign enterprises, tying up their money in solidly conservative commitments which do nothing to develop the national economies.

Given these unfavorable circumstances, it is not surprising that political instability characterizes the whole
region, that dictators flourish, and that the assassination
of a president is a fairly frequent occurrence. Even in
relatively peaceful Costa Rica President José Figueres was
faced with some internal political turbulence as well as
plottings abroad during his term of office (1953-1957).
At almost any given moment at least one Central American country is convinced another one is plotting against
it, often with considerable reason.

Guatemala.   When General Jorge Ubico was finally
overthrown in 1944, one of the most ruthless dictators
left the Central American scene. Since seizing power in
1931 Ubico had accomplished few of the material improvements which are usually cited to justify authoritarian rule. The gravely inadequate education system was
expanded, and a few roads were built which could be used
however only in the dry season, but only a semblance of
economic prosperity was maintained and this was due to
an agreement permitting the free entry of coffee into the
United States. The peace of the grave established by Ubico
definitely did not prepare the way for more democratic
government which is one of the ways by which dictatorship might justify itself.

Juan José Arévalo had been in exile for years, lectur-
ing at Argentine universities, before his term as President
(1945-1951). He began a fundamental social revolution
in Guatemala; abolished forced labor and promulgated an
advanced Labor Code, laid plans for the breakup of large
landholdings, created a Social Security Institute, reorgan-
ized the army in the direction of less authoritarianism,
made several educational improvements, and under his
stimulus the Indians began to participate in government.
His ambivalent attitude toward communism caused some
criticism; he declared against it, but the party was able
to organize swiftly and strongly during his regime.

When Colonel Jacobo Arbenz took the presidential oath
in 1951 before fifty thousand spectators in the national
stadium, an impressive and quite uneconomic structure

which Guatemala could ill afford, the way was paved for further Communist influence in the courts, legislature, and propaganda media. Arbenz announced his objective to be the conversion of Guatemala from a dependent nation with a semi-colonial economy to an economically independent country, and the conversion of its predominantly feudal economy into a modern capitalistic one.

The principal step taken by Arbenz toward these distant goals was the enactment of the controversial Agrarian Reform Law of July 15, 1952, which looked forward to the distribution of expropriated land to some three hundred thousand families. When the U.S. government supported the United Fruit Company in its opposition to the expropriation of its lands without what it regarded as just compensation, a perfect instrument to rouse anti-American spirit was created. When Secretary Dulles insisted on presenting a declaration against international communism at the Tenth Inter-American Congress in Caracas in March, 1954, Guatemala led the fight against imperialism and denounced U.S. policy as that of "the Big Stick, tarnished dollar diplomacy, and the landing of Marines in Latin American ports." After much backstage maneuvering and heated discussion, the declaration was passed by a vote of seventeen to one with two of the most important countries—Argentina and Mexico—abstaining, but the reputation of the United States was not thereby enhanced in Latin America.

Events now moved swiftly. The disclosure on May 17, 1954, that a shipment of arms from Poland was en route to Guatemala led Dulles to fear that a Communist coup was imminent in Guatemala, only two hours distant by air from the Panama Canal. Then in June, 1954, an obscure Guatemalan exile in Honduras, Colonel Carlos Castillo Armas, launched his rebel force against the Arbenz government. Neither the United Nations nor the Organization of American States was called in to move its machinery to avert this threat to peace. Pacification was arranged on July 1 by El Salvador and the United States, and an "unusual feature" of the settlement was the presence of half-a-dozen officers from the U.S. Army, Navy, and Air Force.[2] Arbenz left Guatemala, reportedly

[2] As quoted by A. P. Whitaker, "Guatemala, OAS and U.S.," *Foreign Policy Bulletin*, XXXII (New York, September 1,

was able to deposit $6 million in a Swiss bank, and made
a visit to Prague. Castillo took over, and ever since there
has been a widespread feeling among Latin Americans
that the United States intervened against a popular democratic government because of imperialistic economic interests.

Castillo announced a five-year economic plan—involv-
ing road building, public health, and electrification—revised the agrarian law, encouraged foreign investment,
and stood fast against the Catholic Church's demand to
be recognized as "pre-eminent." His government recognized the need for incorporating the Indians into the
national life[3] and organized a Seminar in June, 1956, to
study the problems of social integration with the help of
specialists from the United States.

Castillo also showed signs of dictatorship, and at one
time had the jails full of prisoners picked up by his vigi-
lante-like secret National Defense Committee Against
Communism. On July 27, 1957, he was killed by a member of the Presidential Guard, apparently a fanatic without political motives. By March, 1958, another president
was sworn in, a conservative career diplomatic officer,
Miguel Ydigoras, elected primarily with the support of
landowners, whose enthusiasm for the agrarian law and
other needed reforms could never be described as more
than luke-warm. Many feared he would become a dictator despite his insistence on his belief in democratic
methods. However this may be, Guatemala today con-
fronts the same basic problems: inadequate transportation, a one-crop economy, a largely illiterate population,
a few wealthy families, which add up to economic and
political instability.

1954), No. 24, p. 5. On this highly disputed event see also
John Gillin and K. H. Silvert, "Ambiguities in Guate-
mala," *Foreign Affairs* (New York, 1956), pp. 469-482;
Julio Adolfo Rey, "Revolution and Liberation: A Review
of Recent Literature on the Guatemalan Situation,"
Hispanic American Historical Review, XXXVIII (1958),
pp. 239-255; and Philip B. Taylor, Jr., "The Guatemalan
Affair: A Critique of United States Foreign Policy,"
American Political Science Review, L (1956), pp. 787-
807.

[3] Gillin and Silvert, "Ambiguities in Guatemala."

It is the second largest and the most populous (3 million inhabitants) of the Central American nations, but Guatemala has not yet been blessed with that benevolent and intelligent dictator called for by Chester Lloyd Jones in his penetrating essay "If I Were Dictator." (*See Reading No. 15.*)

El Salvador. Beset with essentially the same past and the same present problems as Guatemala, this smallest and most densely populated country (2 million inhabitants) of all Central America offers a modestly refreshing contrast to its neighbor, Guatemala. During 1931-1944 the country was ruled by Maximiliano Hernández Martínez, a different kind of military dictator, for he was a Theosophist, who ignored the educated Salvadoreans and appealed directly to the poverty-stricken peons. He devised unusual methods of corn planting which fascinated the agricultural workers but produced no corn. He invented nostrums guaranteeing relief from rheumatism, heart disease, and dysentery. As one imaginative scheme failed, he would concoct an even more captivating project to keep his people interested. But he was a bloody dictator, too, and the frequent uprisings were put down with cruelty. He was once quoted as saying "It is a greater crime to kill an ant than a man, for when a man dies he becomes reincarnated, while an ant dies forever."

When this eccentric dictator was forced to resign in 1944, the usual period of uncertainty set in with a succession of men passing rapidly through the presidency until an army officer, Oscar Osorio, in 1950 promised a period of "honest reconstruction." To almost everybody's surprise, he accomplished just that, seeking to diversify agriculture, stimulate light industry, improve rural living conditions and public health, develop highways, housing, and electrical power, in short, what was officially called the Program of Economic Development and Social Well-being. Osorio also uncovered a Communist plot and destroyed it.

Another army officer, José María Lemus, was the hand-picked candidate of Osorio. He won the fantastic election of 1956 which was chiefly notable because of the refusal of the people to revolt despite a most Gilbert and Sullivan atmosphere. *The New York Times* described it as "by all odds the most rancorous and confused campaign in El Salvador's recent history." Once in power Lemus promised a continuance during his term (1956-1962) of the economic and social reforms of the previous administration and expected to continue taxation of the few wealthy families that control the country economically. Fluctuations in the price of El Salvador's principal export, coffee, poses a fundamental problem and the political situation remains explosive. Lemus' visit to Washington in March, 1959, was considered extremely important to the country. As reported in *The New York Times*, "The great difficulty facing President Lemus is to convince the United States that this small Central American nation could suddenly blow up. His advisers are gathering all available material to buttress his arguments." The impoverishment of the land in this predominantly agricultural country indicates that President Lemus' basic problem will continue to face his successors. (*See Reading No. 15.*) And back of every president stands a coalition of the army and the large landowners.

El Salvador has made one unique and important contribution to the peace of Central America. It has been the home of the movement to promote unity in this badly divided sub-continent. Many efforts for cultural, economic, and political unification have originated in El Salvador, and most of the existing regional organizations make their headquarters in the capital city, San Salvador. At a time when most of its neighbors have been conspiring against one another, El Salvador has maintained an exemplary neutrality. This is worthy of note, for it presages a growing political maturity which has made it possible for it to work toward the peaceful settlement of the many and bitterly contested disputes among the Central American nations. Other nations have participated in the search for Central American unity. Honduras has loudly championed this ideal, and a modest economic step has been taken by the General Tire Company subsidiary in Guatemala which manufactures rubber tires for sale throughout Central America under a regional arrangement. If Central American union ever becomes a reality, however, El Salvador will be recognized as one of its chief architects.

Honduras. With a population approaching 2 million people, this is the Central American "banana republic" par excellence, Bananas are, indeed, its primary export. Revolutions, invasions, and civil wars have been endemic throughout its history; and in General Tiburcio Carías, Honduras produced a dictator who, in his sixteen-year presidency, exhibited all the usual traits of a paternalistic, authoritarian *caudillo*. Yet he was one of the first presidential candidates in Honduras to accept a defeat in open elections (in 1928) without starting a revolution, and when he left office in 1949 he removed himself more completely from the government than anyone anticipated. His conservatism led him to oppose suffrage for women and labor organization, and under his regime democratic institutions withered. Although generally lenient with opponents, he felt that serious lawbreakers should be discouraged and some three hundred prisoners, including some political transgressors, were kept at public work in the capital while chained to heavy balls. With complete power in his hands for many years, he failed to accomplish any resounding material progress.

The years since 1949, when the dictator stepped down in favor of a friend, have been tumultuous. Juan Manuel Gálvez proved during his presidency (1949-1953) to be unexpectedly independent of Carías, and he began some much needed transportation improvements. He also allotted more money to education, supported agricultural diversification to mitigate the unhealthy dependence on bananas, encouraged foreign investment, and even tried to get Hondurans to pay income taxes. Besides laboring for material improvement, Gálvez tried to foster democratic ideals and the long dormant popular desire for freedom. All of his constructive efforts were undermined by the prolonged and expensive controversy with the United Fruit Company in 1954 which led to the first general labor strike in Honduran history. Communists were active, but the longstanding poverty, illiteracy, and disorganization of the workers were enough reasons to provide a fertile ground for agitation for better working and living conditions. Some $15 million worth of bananas ripened and perished, unpicked, but Honduran labor won a position far different from its unorganized subservience under Carías. The question now is whether it will be encouraged to develop a native, anti-Communist leadership or be driven, as elsewhere, into the arms of the Communists.

A second serious blow to President Gálvez's constructive enterprises was the acrimonious and confused election of 1954, which was won by Ramón Villeda. He was not permitted to take office, and for two years thereafter Honduras was governed by decrees issued by the self-appointed "chief of state" Julio Lozano Díaz, who exercised dictatorial powers until forced out by a military junta in October, 1956. The junta governed reasonably well until December 19, 1957, and two days later Villeda was installed as "duly elected constitutional president" for a six-year term. Soon thereafter Villeda and a large group of officials went on a junket to South America, accompanied by a photographer and journalist who later produced an illustrated volume on the expedition. With this fiscal beginning, it is not surprising to learn that by the spring of 1959 teachers remained unpaid, pension payments were in arrears, and bombs exploded frequently at night in the capital Tegucigalpa.

The basic economic and social problems still exist. Yet the picture is not wholly black for, as William S. Stokes has pointed out, even under the successive dictatorships "the average Honduran is to a large extent a free agent." (*See Reading No. 18.*)

Nicaragua. Except for having an American adventurer named William Walker "elected" President in 1856, and having one of the obvious sites for a much-disputed transisthmian canal, Nicaragua's history in the nineteenth century ran the regular course. Relentless warfare between the two political parties was endemic, and during 1893-1909 an unscrupulous dictator, José Santos Zelaya, held brutish sway. The United States intervened both diplomatically and with arms, and for the period 1909-1933 dominated Nicaragua through a customs collectorship and Marines, which led to vigorous Latin American criticism of "dollar diplomacy." Washington found this criticism increasingly embarrassing and Herbert Hoover withdrew the Marines.

Anastasio Somoza quickly rose to power after the Marines left and present-day Nicaragua is largely the result of his work, for good and for evil. Somoza had spent seven years in Philadelphia as a young man, and there developed an enduring respect for the United States and became an ardent follower of the Philadelphia Phillies baseball team. By 1937 Somoza had risen from army chief to the presidency by the strong-arm method and had eliminated the elusive and popular rebel leader Augusto Sandino, by assassination according to many. Once in the saddle he promoted economic development by attracting foreign capital and by encouraging private enterprise. A thorough economic study by an International Bank mission in 1951-1952 produced much useful advice, and both coffee and cotton prices boomed in the 1950's. Roads and ports were improved, electrical power developed, and education increased. Indeed, by 1954 Nicaragua published the news that it had more teachers than soldiers—4,991 to 4,052—a boast that neighboring Costa Rica had been making for years. Hospitals increased, public health services expanded throughout the country, and gross national production grew from $170 million in 1951 to $310 million in 1956. Even though most of Somoza's reform came after 1950, after he had been in complete control for a dozen years, the resulting material benefits were impressive.

His relations with his neighbors, however, particularly Costa Rica, progressively deteriorated. The Organization of American States had to be called in during December, 1948, and for a time hostility ceased. Personal friction continued between Costa Rican President José Figueres and Somoza, who believed that Costa Rica supported Communist plots to kill him. As he considered himself one of the great bulwarks against communism in the Americas, this specter was particularly galling to him. He was shot on September 21, 1956, by a young Nicaraguan who apparently had no other motive than hatred for the dictator. At Somoza's death his son Luis assumed the reins of government and was elected for the 1957-1963 presidential term, while another son, Anastasio, took charge of the National Guard.

Whatever may develop under the rule of Somoza's sons, who are considered to be much less competent than their father, it is clear that an epoch has ended in Nicaraguan history. Somoza's twenty-year domination of the country has raised two questions that have not yet been fully answered, certainly not to everyone's satisfaction. The first is: Why did the United States appear to support this dictator so enthusiastically? The U.S. Ambassador, Thomas

Whelan, a close personal friend, immediately telephoned to Washington when Somoza was shot and, without having received any request from Nicaraguan authorities, urged immediate aid. President Eisenhower at once ordered a medical team from the Canal Zone to fly to Nicaragua and later despatched the commander of the Walter Reed Army Hospital in Washington to join the other U.S. doctors. Despite this array of medical talent Somoza died in Gorgas Hospital in Panama, where he had been transferred for better facilities than were available in Nicaragua.

Reaction to the passing of Somoza varied greatly. Cuba, ruled by his great friend, the dictator Fulgencio Batista, declared three days of mourning, while the Uruguayan parliament passed a resolution honoring the murderer. President Eisenhower roused the ever latent hostility to the United States in Latin America when he expressed his deepest sympathy in what was considered emphatic terms and called the attack "dastardly." Much unnecessary illwill was generated by this extremely solicitous attitude toward one of the most notorious Latin American dictators. After the President's brother, Dr. Milton Eisenhower, made his "fact-finding visit" to Central America in 1958, he strongly advocated that the United States treat dictators with cold correctness, reserving warm *"abrazos"* for democratic leaders in Latin America.

A more difficult question to answer is the second one: What was the nature of Somoza's dictatorship and its accomplishments for the country? He undoubtedly brought Nicaragua political peace, and he was certainly a man of personality and acumen. A chaotic and backward country was given a measure of economic progress. Yet the new roads he built seem ordinarily to lead to or go near one of his many ranches. His private commercial interests included distilleries, sugar mills, cotton gins, lumber, cattle, cement, soap, textiles, ice-making, a steamship line, and even a barber shop. Through these numerous enterprises he was able to build up one of the greatest personal fortunes in the Western Hemisphere, estimated at $60 million, a tremendous sum to have been accumulated in a poor country with about one and a quarter million people. Perhaps the worst blot against his regime was that it did nothing to prepare the people for participation in government. He made all serious decisions; his ministers were glorified clerks. He harshly suppressed democratic opposition, prohibited trade unionism, and was vociferously against freedom of the press. The only dictators who seriously rivaled him in fierce statements against communism were his friends Batista in Cuba and Trujillo in the Dominican Republic.

The future will tell whether economic development and material progress under Somoza were enough to make possible a more liberal regime under his sons.

Costa Rica. This small nation of about one million population has long considered itself in a class apart from the rest of Central America, and its leaders have no hesitation in speaking their minds on hemisphere matters. (*See Readings Nos. 2-3.*) In 1954, for example, Costa Rica opposed holding the Tenth Inter-American Conference in Caracas because a dictatorship was in power in Venezuela, and refused to attend.

Costa Rica has a largely white European population, a high literacy rate, a police force instead of a standing army, and a relatively peaceful history. Her presidents have usually been civilians, and Costa Rica is well ahead of most Latin American countries in political maturity and dedication to liberty. Ever since the election of 1889 there has been a reassuring development in political stability, partly made possible by the existence of widely distributed land holding. Dictators did not flourish, and yet events since 1948 demonstrate that democracy is still somewhat young and insecure in Costa Rica. A revolution occurred in that year when the election of Otilio Ulate was disputed until a young agriculturist named José Figueres led an "Army of National Liberation" to put down those who opposed Ulate. Ulate proved to be an honest president (1948-1953) whose adherence to conservative fiscal policies and devotion to economic development saved Costa Rica from difficult days.

José Figueres was elected to succeed Ulate on a platform emphasizing the need for radical economic policies to make the nation more independent and opposition to the dictatorial regimes in the Caribbean. He won a smashing victory at the polls in a democratic election, was inaugurated in November, 1953, and quickly became one of the most controversial figures in Central American politics. He favored economic expansion through increased productivity, welcomed foreign investment but offered no privileged status, and believed that the United States should support democracy in Latin America by ending aid and encouragement to dictators whether duly elected or not. His greatest triumph was the negotiation of a new contract with the United Fruit Company on June 4, 1954, by which Costa Rica received 35 per cent of the company's net earnings instead of 15 per cent. This contract symbolized a new and constructive step that brought positive benefits to both parties and had repercussions in other banana-producing countries.

In other fields President Figueres won few laurels and much criticism. Scandals broke out from time to time, his relations with Somoza went from bad to worse, and ex-President Ulate broke with him. Mario Echandi won the 1958 election and in his inaugural address called for "the advance of the working class" to assure Costa Rica of a stable democracy. But the coolness of the upper classes to this goal does not augur well and further achievements in civic cooperation will be necessary if Costa Rica is to maintain her honored position among the democratic leaders of Latin America.

Costa Rica has been usually described in glowing terms; it is a model democracy, a land of peace and progress far different from her Central American neighbors. To a real extent this is true, but it is also true that sociological investigations reveal that Costa Rica has much in common with other Latin American countries: "The class structure with emphasis on manual labor as an important factor in determining status; the notion of "first families"; the subordination of women; the superior prestige of professional life rather than business; the great interest in politics, a politics of personalities rather than issues; the idealization of democracy; the "easy" Catholicism; the valuing of the life of "culture" rather than of technology; the disinclination to join clubs or civic enterprises—these are some of the features of Costa Rican life which help us to know Latin America generally." [4]

Costa Ricans are proud of their democratic traditions

[4] John and Mavis Biesanz, *Costa Rican Life,* New York: Columbia University Press, 1944, p. viii. The statement quoted was made by Robert Redfield.

and indignant when corruption creeps into their political life. They also recognize the ills of their country, which another sociologist describes thus: "The red tile roofs of the little villages are picturesque, yet many shelter homes where half the children die of stomach trouble or malaria, where the father's earnings in the coffee groves or cane fields buy little more than beans, rice, and tortillas, where clothes are shabby and blankets inadequate for the chilly nights. The country has more teachers than soldiers, but the teachers are underpaid and in the schools there are ten times as many in the first grade as in the sixth. Literacy is as high as it is in any Latin American country; nevertheless, the gap between the uneducated peon and the son of his wealthy employer is wider than ever before. Ticos are friendly and sociable, yet they are individualists and rarely cooperate for common ends. The girls strolling in the *retreta* [park promenade] are pretty, but they have a world of masculine prejudice and pride to conquer before they achieve a higher status. There is great pride of family, but little concern for illegitimacy, prostitution, and venereal diseases. The soil is fertile; still many are underfed. Coffee is a 'grain of gold' to some, while it keeps others poor and dependent. Although land ownership is widespread, many of the registered properties are mere scraps of land big enough for a house, while in other cases, many land units are owned by one man." [5]

These basic problems are being slowly met in Costa Rica, but more rapidly than in any other Central American country.

Panama. This small country with about a million people, the geographic center of the Americas, has as its principal crop the revenues it derives from the Canal Zone. Politics and economics revolve around this single topic. In spite of widespread anti-Yankee feeling and resentment against racist and domineering attitudes displayed by U.S. officials and citizens in the Zone (*see Reading No. 19*), communism has not found fertile soil in Panama. Waves of nationalism break over the country periodically: political passions are nowhere more intense or divisive. All the classic problems of Central American republics are present: a one-crop export (bananas), illiteracy, poverty, housing deficiencies, insufficient electric

[5] *Ibid.*, pp. 252-253.

power, and unstable political institutions. Revolutionary
outbursts and bloody riots have been common during the
past ten years; not one of the last six presidents served a
full term in office.

At this strategic crossroad of world trade, the atomic
age and the ancient life of the jungle live practically cheek
by jowl. The rural districts are centuries away in culture
from the world of the modern office buildings in the
capital and the jet bombers of the Zone. As late as 1925
a Smithsonian anthropologist on an expedition in the back
country led Indians in revolt and was proclaimed Em-
peror of Darién.

Panama was able to establish and maintain its independence from Colombia in 1903 because of U.S. support. The great canal, after its opening in 1914, became
the outstanding fact of Panamanian life. One third of all
Panamanian revenue derives from the Zone, through income paid by the U.S. government for the lease of this
50-mile waterway which cost originally $366 million, and
through wages paid Zone employees, or expenditures by
U.S. personnel assigned to the Zone. Without the Canal,
Panamanians would live meagerly from the sale of their
bananas.

Political decisions in Panama have been made by a
few powerful families, by shifting political combinations,
by the national police, at times by the clamor of an
aroused populace, and often by American authorities. The
United States resorted to armed intervention until 1918
and since then has tried diplomatic pressure. Panama improved her position by the Treaty of 1936 by which the
United States formally terminated Panama's protectorate
status, agreed not to intervene, raised the annual payment
for lease of the Zone from $250,000 to $430,000, and
met other Panamanian demands.

Despite this treaty, relations between the two countries
continued to be uncertain. The Axis-supporter Arnulfo
Arias was president for a time (1940-1941) and then
returned to win the election of 1949, when the strong
support of police chief José Antonio Remón more than
made up for his unsavory past. But this strange combina-
tion fell apart, and for four years Remón installed and
removed presidents with lightning rapidity. When he had
himself legally elected president in 1952, many Pana-

manians had misgivings but, until his career was cut short by assassination in January, 1955, his policies were sound. Assisted by his energetic and politically conscious wife Cecilia, he achieved political tranquillity for Panama, introduced higher income taxes and other realistic economic improvements, kept an eye on the Communists, and won a substantial victory by negotiating a new treaty with the United States, signed and ratified in 1955 after sixteen months of difficult but generally amicable discussions. The United States agreed by this treaty to pay $1,930,000 as annual rent instead of the 1936 figure of $430,000, agreed to limit some of the Zone business activities which competed with Panamanian commerce, and agreed to abolish the hated double standard in wages by accepting for the first time the principle of one basic wage scale for all the U.S. and Panamanian employees in the Zone. Panama in return made available twenty thousand acres for training and military maneuvers.

Although President Remón was killed before the treaty was formally approved, his influence was the dominant one in Panama's achievement of long wished for improvements in relations with the United States. And the State Department demonstrated that it was willing to negotiate with a small country, even though events in other parts of the world apparently were also partly responsible. Panama, too, has learned to use a very effective weapon—international public opinion. Panama's position has been dramatized to the world, for their delegates to youth congresses, athletic meetings, and labor conferences, all have something to say on "Yankee Imperialism" and "Racial Discrimination" in the Canal Zone.

Following the murder of Remón, Panamanian affairs became swiftly disorganized. Vice-President José Ramón Quizado was accused and finally convicted of complicity in the crime and Second Vice-President Ricardo Arias was sworn in as president, staying in office until Ernesto de la Guardia, Jr., won the regular election in May, 1956. He was inaugurated during the excitement and bitterness that again flared up when the United States ignored Panama during the Suez crisis of 1956. Secretary Dulles chose to exclude Panama from the London Conference, which led Panama to adhere with ten Communist and neutralist nations to a plan opposed to the "international control" proposed in London. Then Dulles went on to reopen old wounds when he not only stated at a press conference that the United States "has rights of sovereignty over the Panama Canal" but also alleged these rights were enjoyed by the United States "to the entire exclusion of the exercise by the Republic of Panama of any such sovereign rights, power, or authority." On top of all this, Panama accused Zone authorities of noncompliance with the 1955 agreement to end discrimination in wages.

Thus the two nations found themselves at loggerheads, and the Canal remained an omnipresent and black shadow in the Panamanian world. Only a small hard core of Panamanians argue for the ultimate ousting of the United States from the Zone, but one American reporter states that "the attitude of many Panamanians, in and out of official position, is that the United States took advantage of Panama's immaturity in 1903 in the original treaty and has continued to do so ever since. Therefore, they feel it only their right to fight continually for 'renegotiations' of the treaty and to assert their basic sovereignty over the zone." And an American sociologist points out that the United States has met "the challenge of hills and jungles with courage, skill, and intelligence" but has not yet learned how to handle successfully the social challenges produced by the head-on collision of Panamanian and American culture. The U.S. official position is that the Canal was built as a service to the shipping of the world, and not as a moneymaker for anyone; running expenses are barely met by the toll charges, and of the billion and a half dollars spent on the Canal the United States has thus far recovered only about one billion.

Panama's recent decision to extend its territorial limits 12 miles to sea may indicate that it is maneuvering into a position of strength from which to renegotiate the treaty once more. Since the United States has rights according to the present treaty only 3 miles seaward from the great waterway, traffic through the canal might be harried or demoralized if Panama should attempt—as it has been hinted it may—to stop ships passing through its territorial water approaching the Canal entrance for customs or maritime formalities.

If international relations remain clouded, internal progress appears uncertain. President de la Guardia has encountered a general public lethargy to any substantial reforms in taxation, rural development, health, and social security. As one sympathetic observer puts it, his administration is "not a precursor to economic reforms but rather the continuation of the outmoded practices and customs of past decades. The list of needs is staggering. It includes agricultural diversification, electrification, increased tourist facilities, expanded education, improved housing and public health, light industrialization, additional road construction, and social enlightenment. It will be years before any one of these problems can be coped with satisfactorily." [6]

The Future of Central America. Political instability is likely to be a source of concern for a long time to come. Vigorous and enlightened leaders of the type of Oscar Osorio in El Salvador and the late José Antonio Remón of Panama can do much to alter the general picture. And if the United States adopts a policy of cool correctness toward dictators, future Somozas may work toward developing political maturity as well as material progress in order to be in the good graces of the United States.

Some benefits may be obtained for all countries by putting into effect some of the long-cherished dreams of Central American union, at least in the economic field. The unfortunate effects of the rigid national boundaries, the small individual markets, and the confusion of tariffs which immensely complicate trade crossing so many borders may be mitigated by the pact signed in 1957 to create a free trade zone and a system of regional industries. In 1958 plans were laid for a regional university, a normal school, polytechnic school, and an agricultural school. Whether these projects will be put into effect remains to be seen. Since 1838 the Central American republics have gone their separate ways, and all attempts at union face formidable obstacles.

Another constructive step is the recent attempt of the United Fruit Company to mend its social fences. Central Americans may not be overly impressed with the company's record of leaving seven dollars in every country

[6] John D. Martz, *Central America. The Crisis and the Challenge,* Chapel Hill: University of North Carolina Press, 1959, p. 318.

for every dollar it takes out in profit, or by its practice of paying higher wages than local employers. More convincing changes to Latin Americans are its recognition of labor unions, obedience to the national laws, its abandonment of the old swashbuckling tactics, its agricultural school, and above all its willingness to negotiate such a favorable contract with President Figueres of Costa Rica.

A final question remains and can only be posed, not answered. Will the politically and economically important people of Central America play their part? Such an experienced and sympathetic student as the late Chester Lloyd Jones raised this fundamental issue in 1934 when he stated that their major problems "continue to be as they have been in the past—little as they themselves and foreign observers have at time recognized this fact—primarily domestic and not foreign problems. Their future—economic, social, and political—turns in all but slight degree on what their peoples can do for themselves, not on influences from outside the national borders." [7] One observer today in Central America considers the "appalling lack of civic responsibility, except perhaps in Costa Rica," as the greatest danger there. "The distressing fact is that unless the privileged few work for the benefit of all, they are going to make worse the present difficult conditions and thereby invite their own destruction."

If the many fundamental problems facing Central America are to be solved, the people and government of the six republics and the United States might well keep in mind the noble words which Secretary of State Elihu Root delivered before the National Assembly of Panama on September 21, 1906, on the subject of the achievement of the Panama Canal: "The work is difficult and delicate; the two peoples, the Anglo-American and the Spanish-American, are widely different in their traditions, their laws, their customs, their methods of thinking and speaking and doing business. It often happens that we misunderstand each other; it often happens that we fail to appreciate your good qualities and that you fail to appreciate ours; and that with perfectly good intentions, with the best of purposes and kindliest of feelings, we clash, we fail to understand each other, we get at cross purposes,

[7] Chester Lloyd Jones, *Costa Rica and Civilization in the Caribbean,* San José, Costa Rica, 1941, p. 151.

and misconception and discord are liable to arise. Let us
remember this in all our intercourse; let us be patient
with each other; let us believe in the sincerity of our
mutual good purposes and kindly feelings, and be patient
and forbearing each with the other, so that we may go
on together in the accomplishment of this great enterprise." [8]

— 2 —

THE CARIBBEAN

Paradise or Poorhouse?   The development of cheap
air transportation, the discovery of that effective insect
destroyer DDT, and the rapid establishment of tourist
facilities have made the Caribbean one of America's favorite areas of relaxation. The tourists who visit the islands stretching 2,000 miles from Central America eastward to the Lesser Antilles discover a tropical playground
which provides the beauty and isolation of the South Sea
Islands a few air hours from the mainland. They are inclined to call it a paradise, as did Columbus when he first
landed. Closer and longer acquaintance leads to a radically different conclusion. The Caribbean islands did, indeed, enjoy a period of grandeur in the seventeenth and
eighteenth centuries when they were among the finest
prizes of empire, with the European nations vying to obtain the famous "sugar islands," but they languished
nearly forgotten during the nineteenth and early twentieth centuries.

Only in the last twenty or thirty years have the islands
emerged from their backward role, but they still have far
to go before a reasonable standard of living is achieved

[8] Robert Bacon and James Brown Scott, eds., *Latin America
   and the United States. Addresses by Elihu Root*, Cambridge, Mass., 1917, pp. 149-151.

for the millions of poor, disease-ridden, illiterate people who constitute a large section of the population in many of the islands. Most of them work on the land, are of Negro descent, and have a very small income. Although important changes have occurred in some of the islands in recent years, these lands of sugar, coffee, bananas, cacao, and tobacco hold a population characterized by its depressed standard of living. So many have left the British territories for England that race riots broke out in London in 1958, and so many Puerto Ricans migrate to New York—though Puerto Rico enjoys a relatively high standard of living—that Manhattan has more Puerto Ricans than San Juan. It was President Herbert Hoover who, injudiciously perhaps but truthfully, described the Caribbean some years ago as a poorhouse, and the basic economic and social conditions there have not radically changed today though substantial improvements are under way in some areas.

Cuba: Rich Land, Poor People.   Fernando Ortiz, Cuba's grand old man of letters, describes his country as a "mixture of cuisines, of races, and of cultures. A thick broth of civilization which bubbles on the Caribbean fire." (*See Reading No. 20.*) Its vast blend of Spanish, Negro, Oriental, and other cultures, he feels, "overshadows in importance every other historical phenomenon." Another distinguishing feature of Cuban life is the dominance of sugar in her economy. Four-fifths or more of Cuba's export revenue is from sugar, for tobacco has declined to a poor second, and the national economy which supports more than 6 million Cubans is highly sensitive to the price of sugar in the world market, to which Cuba is the principal supplier. José Martí, the Cuban national hero, recognized the dangers of monoculture when he wrote, in 1883: "A people commits suicide the day on which it bases its existence on a single crop." Agricultural diversification has made real headway in the last twenty years and the tourist industry steadily increases. But sugar is still King in Cuba.

A third basic element in Cuba's past, present, and future is its proximity to the United States. Here is her principal market for her sugar, and Cuba buys much of her goods from the United States. Although Cuba was of political concern to the United States throughout the nine-

teenth century, it was only after the Spanish American
War that a direct relationship came. After a period of
American military rule 1898-1902, Cuba was free but
not free to make her own mistakes, for the Platt Amendment gave the United States the right to intervene. This
"philanthropic Yankee imperialism" was bitterly resented
in Cuba, and when President Gerardo Machado was
finally deposed in 1933, after eleven years of murder and
oppression under what Cubans considered was virtual
American protection, the hated amendment was finally
abrogated in 1934.

Cuba passed brusquely from the era of the Platt
Amendment to the era of Fulgencio Batista, which was
terminated only in January, 1959. This one-time sergeant
rose to power in the confusion that followed the overthrow of Machado who, even if he had undertaken such
useful projects as the 700-mile Central Highway, had
also indulged in such extravagances as the $18 million
marble capitol building in Havana. Merely a stenographer
at army headquarters when the dictator fell, Batista organized an enlisted men's revolt which helped to over-
turn the provisional government that replaced Machado's
regime. The sergeant-stenographer quickly consolidated
his control of the army, the classic instrument of dictators. Soon almost all the higher officers owed their positions to him, and he provided substantial benefits for the
enlisted men as well; he raised their pay, built excellent
barracks, furnished good uniforms and excellent food,
provided recreation fields, and established pension funds.
He also cultivated organized labor successfully and used
patronage profusely to control civilian leaders. Only some
of the intellectuals and university students grumbled much
against his regime.

For seven years he ruled through puppets, seven in
number, and in 1940 assumed the presidency himself. His
four-year term was marked by good government—at least,
it seemed better than Cuba had ever had before. With
sugar prices steady during the war years, Batista was able
to expand public works vigorously—roads, bridges, har-
bor installations, and power plants. Public business was
conducted expeditiously, education was improved, the
press was relatively unfettered, and few political crimes
were perpetrated despite the persistent strain of violence

in Cuban politics. When Batista permitted Dr. Ramón Grau San Martín to be elected in 1944, he was able to retire to live in Florida with both a large private fortune and the good will of many Cubans.

Neither Grau San Martín, indicted in Cuban courts for allegedly misappropriating $178 million during his administration, nor his successor, Carlos Prío Socarrás (1948-1952), was able to withstand the temptations of the presidency, and in 1952 Batista again seized power through a barracks conspiracy. Now a thorough dictatorship was imposed which became increasingly harsh. Congress was indefinitely dissolved, although its members were kept on the payroll. The press was muzzled, the University closed, and groups of exiled Cubans in New York, Mexico, and elsewhere began to plot Batista's downfall. In December, 1956, Fidel Castro and a dozen youths landed on the eastern end of the island to begin a dogged and ever-increasing opposition, and eventually the rebel forces drove Batista out. "Rich beyond the wildest dreams of the biggest U.S. business man," Batista took refuge in Dictator Trujillo's Dominican Republic.

The coming to power of Fidel Castro led to strained relations with the United States, for the rebels resented the support given by the United States to Batista throughout most of his rule and felt that U.S. ambassadors had been unnecessarily friendly to this tough and brutal dictator. This bitterness was compounded when some U.S. Congressional and other voices were raised to condemn the manner of the executions Fidel Castro approved for Batista's worst henchmen.

The future is far from clear. Fidel Castro's relative youth and lack of experience in civil government will be tested severely by the many problems left in the wake of the dictator. As Herbert L. Matthews, the veteran *New York Times* Latin American expert, reported: "Those who fought against General Batista believed that they fought for liberty, democracy, and decent government. It remains for the coming months to prove whether they, like their fathers who fought against the dictator of the Nineteen Twenties, Gerardo Machado, have fought in vain or whether a new era is really beginning for Cuba."

Meanwhile Cuba still is located so close to the United States that the island feels profoundly the effects of its neighbor's economy. Sugar still occupies half of the cultivated land, employs a quarter of the labor force, and provides 85 per cent of exports by value, including such by-products as rum, molasses, alcohol, and syrups. Of the half million Cubans who work in the sugar fields or mills, only about 12 per cent have year-round jobs; the others work four months or less, and eke out a precarious living by subsistence farming. The great landed estates are held by a few corporations, largely foreign, and half of the billion dollar sugar industry is estimated to be in American hands.

Projects for diversification of crops have made some progress; cattle raising has developed, rice production has increased fourfold since 1945, and vegetable growing for the American market has begun. Cuba's forest resources have been wastefully depleted, however, and the abundance of fish in her coastal waters has not yet been seriously touched. Above all Cuban problems towers the unsolved land riddle. Many Cuban leaders, among them Batista, have discussed proposals for forcing idle lands into cultivation by increased taxation and have even drafted legislation for the distribution of land, on small payments, to landless farmers; but few Cubans have received land. "Land reform" by itself will not guarantee a higher level of living in Cuba. Vocational training for agricultural workers will be required as well as a greatly expanded educational system, improved sanitation, and a better diet for the rural masses. One favorable development is the definite indication of a steady decline in the birth rate.

Almost immediately after his triumphal entry into Havana Fidel Castro announced that he would give immediate consideration to land reform. If he can win this battle he will have accomplished a feat greater than his success against Batista, for Cuban land problems are ancient and resistant to change. (*See Reading No. 21.*)

Trujillo's Land, and Haiti. Immediately eastward from Cuba lies an island with over more than 5 million people, divided into two separate nations, the western third occupied by the Negro republic Haiti and the rest under the rule of one of the most notorious Latin American dictators of all time, Generalissimo Rafael Trujillo.

Columbus established here the first city in America,

now called Ciudad Trujillo, and for the first half century of Spanish rule Hispaniola was a key area in the empire. Then the more spectacular conquests of Mexico and Peru turned the island into a poor way-station, harassed by European rivals. Eventually the island was ceded to France, and in 1804 the French-speaking western end won its independence under the dramatic Negro leader and ex-slave Toussaint L'Ouverture. Four decades later the eastern two-thirds of the island won its freedom as the Dominican Republic. The record of both countries during the nineteenth century was a dismal story of almost continuous tumult, confusion, and tyranny. The early years of the twentieth century brought fiscal supervision by the United States and rule by Marines in both countries, for the United States feared that the anarchy in the island would enable European powers to gain a fresh foothold in the Caribbean and that American investments would be imperiled.

When the occupation ended, in 1930 in the Dominican Republic and in 1934 in Haiti, the United States was disillusioned concerning its ability to govern the island. Some good had doubtless been accomplished, although the methods and achievements differed somewhat in the two countries, but Dominicans and Haitians alike celebrated the disappearance of U.S. rule as their second emancipation.

Haiti has not suffered any long-time strong men but instead a succession of weak and transient dictators, with the Garde d'Haiti often the directing force. Nor has it a one-crop economy. Rather its fundamental economic problem, to quote from a 1949 United Nations investigation, "derives from relentless pressure of a steadily growing, insufficiently educated population upon limited, vulnerable and—so far as agricultural land is concerned— alarmingly shrinking natural resources." When this surplus population attempted to work in Cuba's sugar harvesting, Batista's hostility to any increase in African blood for Cuba ended this immigration. When Haitians flocked across the Dominican border for work, Trujillo resorted to the killing of an estimated 10,000 to 20,000 Haitians, for he was determined to make his domain a "white" nation.

Haiti has come to be one of the most isolated nations

in the New World. French-speaking Haitians maintain
cultural relations with France, with its traditional racial
tolerance, while economically Haiti is closely connected
with the United States. The majority of the over 3 million
densely packed-in people are further isolated by the nation's caste system, for they have no effective link with
their own intellectual and social elite. (*See Reading No.
22.*)

The tempo of instability has increased in recent years.
Between December 5, 1956, and May 25, 1957, four governments succeeded one another more rapidly than at any
time since 1804. These hectic 170 days resulted in a chaos
which left Haiti even more impoverished than before the
U.S. occupation.

The explosive nature of Caribbean politics and the
chain reactions sometimes developing there may be seen
in the situation existing in March, 1959. The Cuban hero
Fidel Castro announced the aim of toppling all dictatorships in the area, an aim supported by President Rómulo
Betancourt of Venezuela, and an estimated 120,000 Haitians are in exile in the Oriente province of Cuba from
which Castro launched his war against Batista. Trujillo
fears that the Cuban government will aid these Haitian
refugees to arm and surge across the 50-mile stretch of
water separating Cuba from Haiti. If this invasion takes
place, will Trujillo in turn invade Haiti as a preventative
action against what he may interpret as a Fidel Castro
threat?

Meanwhile the United States finds itself in its standard
dilemma. It does not consider the present Haitian government the most desirable or most perfect type, but its overthrow might cause even more economic distress to the
poverty-ridden Haitians than they now endure. So the
United States backs the present government of Dr. Fran-
çois Duvalier in Haiti with a $6 million loan from the
International Cooperation Administration, and a U.S.
military mission of Marines was authorized to go to Haiti
at the invitation of President Duvalier, whose power is
all but absolute in Haiti. If he should fall, the United
States would find itself once more in the embarrassing
position of backing a loser in Latin America.

The American occupation of the Dominican Republic
did not noticeably advance political democracy there, and

it roused much antagonism toward the United States in Latin America and resulted in the organization of a trained constabulary force which enabled Rafael L. Trujillo to spring to power in 1930. He demonstrated his organization when a hurricane struck shortly after he was inaugurated, and thereafter went on from one triumphant success to another. Public health advances have been notable, illiteracy reduced, transportation improved and, as Hubert Herring states: "No other Latin American ruler offers a more eloquent record of material achievement. He took over in 1930 a nation in which lawlessness, banditry, and civil strife had prevailed since its birth in 1844; today there is transquility, and country roads are as safe as those in Iowa. In 1930 the republic was bankrupt and poverty-ridden, with a foreign debt of more than $20,-000,000 and a total national income of about $7,000,000; by 1953 foreign and domestic debts had been liquidated, and the national income had exceeded $300,000,000—according to Trujillo's statisticians. For more than twenty years the government budget had been balanced, and in 1954 it had reached the record high of $96,000,000. Sales in the world market stood at more than $100,000,000, about half from sugar and two-fifths from cacao and coffee.

"Impressive buildings and public works further attest Trujillo's skill. Ciudad Trujillo is smartly modern and boasts excellent public buildings and private homes, as well as one of the finest tourist hotels in the Caribbean." [9] On top of all this Trujillo's paid advertisements in U.S. newspapers stress his unwavering stand against communism and his aid to Jews by establishing a highly publicized colony of European refugees at Sosúa, though few apparently cared to stay.

The blessings of the "Era of Trujillo" have been bought at a heavy price. The Dominican press is controlled, critics of the regime are denounced as Communists, the army is kept content with largesse, and the highly effective Dominican police are in strict control. Large numbers of the Generalissimo's family are on the national payroll, and only his great friend, the late satrap of Nicaragua, Anastasio Somoza, rivaled him in the variety and extent of his

[9] Hubert Herring, *A History of Latin America,* New York: Alfred A. Knopf, 1955, p. 430.

profitable commercial enterprises. Loyalty to Trujillo is an absolute requirement. Persons entering upon a government job or joining the Army swear loyalty to Trujillo, not to the Constitution. Each August 16, on the anniversary of the Generalissimo's assumption of power, the newspapers of the capital city Ciudad Trujillo are filled with congratulatory telegrams and rapturous reports on progress under the guidance of *El Benemérito,* who is proclaimed "Not a Man: A National Symbol" in lush Byzantine prose. (*See Reading No. 23.*)

Trujillo has been particularly desirous of ensuring loyalty in recent years. When Professor Jesús de Galíndez, a well-known refugee from Franco's Spain, disappeared in New York in March, 1956, some Americans, including Congressmen, ascribed the responsibility to Trujillo. The case quickly became a *cause célèbre,* with the Dominican government employing such lawyers and public relations experts as Morris Ernst at a reputed cost of half a million dollars a year to represent it in the United States. It became a controversial issue between the U.S. and Dominican governments, and relations were further strained when General Rafael Trujillo, Jr., now Chief of Staff of the Dominican Army, was denied a diploma by a U.S. Army college for failure to fulfill the requirements.

Meanwhile the Generalissimo continues his rule, and extended shelter to Perón and Batista when their people drove them out. Whether his long period of peace has meant much to the common man in economic terms, and whether the dictatorship helped to prepare the Dominican people for the perils of a nonauthoritarian regime will be discovered later.

Puerto Rico: Operation Bootstrap. When Nelson Rockefeller, wise in the mores of Latin Americans, successfully campaigned for the governorship of New York in 1958 he spoke in Spanish to the Puerto Ricans in Manhattan and often had his wife and family with him at political rallies. It was a clear recognition of the political significance of the Puerto Ricans who have steadily migrated to the United States during the last twenty years. The 35 movie houses in upper Manhattan that show only Spanish language films is another indication of their importance. And the fact that waves of people seeking better jobs than their homeland afforded could migrate to the United States freely points to one of the unique developments in the Caribbean today. The government of Puerto Rico has employed so many of the modern advertising techniques that it is difficult to strike a just balance in assessing what Puerto Rico's first popularly elected governor Luis Muñoz Marín has described as "Operation Bootstrap."

The period of confusion and uncertainty in Puerto Rico after the acquisition of this island by the United States following the Spanish American War did not promise much. Without mineral resources, Puerto Rico presented the familiar pattern of the densely populated, underdeveloped tropical area where, of all the important indices, only the population showed a sustained and uninterrupted growth. Agricultural improvements and land distribution had only limited value, for no matter how well tilled or how equitably divided, the cultivated land could not possibly support the growing population. In addition, Puerto Rico faced the problem of maintaining her own cultural identity in the face of powerful and pervasive U.S. influences, and of deciding politically whether she aimed at independence, statehood, or something else. The island made gradual progress toward self-government during the years 1898-1952 during which it was "an unincorporated territory" of the United States.

The political tempo increased in 1938 with the establishment of the Popular Democratic Party, which provided Muñoz Marín with an ever-growing political base and enabled him to undertake many economic reforms. During World War II Puerto Rico, strategically located at the gateway to the Caribbean and the Panama Canal, became a military bastion through feverish construction of military bases which brought jobs, money, trade—and attention. By 1948 Muñoz Marín took office as the first elected native governor, and economic and social development followed. Industries were attracted from the mainland by temporary tax exemptions and low wages for labor. Public health facilities so improved that life expectancy increased from 46 in 1940 to 61 years in 1952, and education became a significant part of Puerto Rico's progress culminating in the University of Puerto Rico under the dynamic direction of Rector Jaime Benítez. The

University has signed an agreement with the U.S. Atomic Energy Commission for a $2,500,000 center, where instruction will be in Spanish, in order to hasten—in President Eisenhower's words—"the beneficial use of nuclear forces throughout the hemisphere."

In 1950 the U.S. Congress, through Public Law 600, provided the basis for a decisive political step by "fully recognizing the principle of consent and approved that principle in a compact subject to agreement by the people of Puerto Rico." This act ushered in a period of intense political and constitutional activity which led to the adoption on March 3, 1952, by a vote of 375,000 to 83,000, of a Constitution establishing the Commonwealth (*Estado Libre Asociado*) of Puerto Rico, which was promptly ratified in Washington.

Thus began a unique experiment in American constitutional development, for Puerto Rico is neither "territory" nor "possession," neither state nor independent republic. No taxes are collected in the island for the benefit of the U.S. Treasury, and Puerto Rico has no voting representation in Congress. Puerto Ricans continue to be U.S. citizens, and foreign relations are conducted by the Department of State. Puerto Rico, according to its able leader Muñoz Marín, neither seeks statehood nor wishes to give up its basic Latin American way of life. (*See Reading No. 24.*) It cherishes its Spanish language and literature and cultivates its cultural heritage through such institutions as the government sponsored Instituto de Cultura Puertorriqueña and its University.

Puerto Rico is proud that distinguished Spanish refugees such as the late Juan Ramón Jiménez and Pablo Casals chose to live in Puerto Rico and that many Latin Americans who are exiled from their own countries have considered this island as a residence "well-suited to the spirit of a free man." They are also proud of their women leaders—of Nilita Vientós Gastón who directs the cultural center, Ateneo Puertorriqueño, with independence and distinction, and of the political know-how of the Mayoress of San Juan, Felisa Rincón de Gautier. Under the skillful management of Arturo Morales Carrión, Under Secretary of State, Puerto Rico has become a training center for technical assistance students. Hundreds of engineers, educators, labor leaders, and administrators have come each year from Latin America, Asia, and Africa to acquire a first-hand knowledge of how Puerto Rico and the United States work together.

The political pot is bubbling, in addition to the economic and cultural development. Governor Muñoz Marín's party still has a comfortable margin of lead. At the other end of the political spectrum are the nationalists, a fringe group with a very small following, who made the newspapers in 1954 when some of their members went to Washington and shot five Congressmen. The Independentista Party, with adherents from many classes, stands for planned and nonviolent political separation. Then there is the Statehood Party, affiliated with the U.S. Republican Party, with much strength among the rising bourgeoisie. It ran Luis Ferré, a dynamic industrialist, against Muñoz Marín in 1952 and came out second.

The issue of statehood vs. comonwealth status seems to overshadow the independence question. Certainly independence would pose a grave economic crisis for the island, which now is one of the few areas in the Caribbean where economic development roughly parallels the growth of population. But leaders of both political parties in Washington have made it clear that the United States would quickly grant independence to the island if it ever became certain that a majority of the Puerto Rican people favored separation.

The achievement of statehood by Alaska and Hawaii has bolstered the hopes of the Statehood Party, but it may be that Muñoz Marín has taken Puerto Rico so far along the Commonwealth path that the voters will not turn back. Much depends upon what happens when he steps aside and his party is faced with the task of maintaining unity without his strong and able hand. The future will also test the strength of Puerto Rico's economic institutions and political maturity. Unless her birth rate declines, her population of over 2,300,000 will find it difficult to attain higher living standards, for unchecked fertility "will ravage the land like a hurricane or a tidal wave." Will industries continue to flow to Puerto Rico when their tax exemptions end, and will the migration to Manhattan flow on in spite of possible recessions in the economy of the United States? Unless the answer is yes to these questions,

"Operation Bootstrap" may run into heavy weather. Meanwhile Puerto Rican political leaders are proud to be the creators of the plan for a commonwealth in voluntary association with the United States.

Other Areas. The Caribbean was the cockpit of America during the three centuries after Columbus, and the British, Dutch, and French sections there today reflect this historical fact. They are scattered over the huge Caribbean area, from British Honduras in Central America to the Guianas on the South American continent. About 4 million people live in the British territories with perhaps another million in all the other areas combined. Most of them suffer from low wages, a low standard of living, and substandard housing. During the last twenty years smallpox, typhus, cholera, sleeping-sickness, and yellow fever have been wiped out; typhoid, tuberculosis, and malaria have been greatly reduced. For people under 50, illiteracy has almost disappeared in the Dutch West Indies, Martinique, and some of the British islands. Paradoxically the region has a high percentage of unemployment and a shortage of technical workers. Almost 100,000 have migrated from British areas to the United Kingdom in recent years, including a considerable number of the relatively few trained workers.

Most of the European sections have slight relations with their mainland Latin American neighbors and differ from them in two respects: (1) their people are preponderantly of African stock with an appreciable percentage of Asiatics; (2) they have remained in association with the European powers but most of them have moved or are moving toward complete political autonomy without revolution or bloodshed.

They have various constitutional relations with the European powers. Martinique and Guadeloupe are departments of France and have a relationship similar to any other French Department. Surinam (Dutch Guiana), like the Netherlands Antilles, has become a partner in the Kingdom of the Netherlands and since the ratification of the 1955 constitution has enjoyed autonomy in internal affairs. The British islands and mainland territories, although still colonies of Britain, exercise varying degrees of internal autonomy. Through the British Caribbean Federation, inaugurated in April, 1958, the islands are mov-

ing toward dominion status. The mainland territories,
British Honduras and British Guiana, are not yet in the
Federation, for they believe that their destinies may lie
with their continental neighbors rather than with the
widely dispersed islands. Jamaica threatens to quit the
Federation and tariff barriers continue to hamper trade,
but even during this pioneer period some progress toward
Federation objectives has been made.

The economies of all the European areas are basically
agricultural except for the island of Trinidad, which derives 35 per cent of its export revenue from oil; Surinam,
where the exportation of bauxite accounts for 80 per cent
of all export receipts; and the Netherlands Antilles, where
petroleum made up 99 per cent of exports in 1956. Elsewhere, sugar is usually the principal crop, although other
products are being developed, such as bananas, citrus
fruits, cocoa, and coffee. Since 1956 mining has assumed
great importance in the economy of Jamaica, British
Guiana, and Surinam. But sugar still provides the bulk
of the income in most countries and is the greatest employer of labor. Since World War II the production of
sugar in the British islands has increased steadily, reach-
ing a record output of 1,000,000 tons in 1955. Two thirds
of this output benefits from a negotiated price under the
Commonwealth Sugar Agreement of £40 a ton as compared with £12 a ton before the war.

The area as a whole, however, has been moving into
the industrial age in an effort to meet its new responsibilities of self-government and to provide employment for
its growing population. Traditionally it produced raw
materials for the metropolitan powers and was discouraged from setting up industries or even growing its own
food. The war changed all this, and the Caribbean Commission—since 1946 including representatives of the three
European powers and the United States—worked to improve both food production and the general situation of
the area.

The results have been significant in the development of
fishing, forest products, mining, and a wide range of light
industries. The British team of industrialists who visited
the British areas in 1953 were impressed by the extent to
which industry, attracted by various kinds of concessions
similar to those utilized in Puerto Rico's "Operation

Bootstrap," had developed, and they predicted steady expansion at a rate that would double the present industrial output in ten years.

Additional capital and more trained workers will be required to achieve this goal. Technical and vocational education is now being stressed, particularly in Trinidad, and apprenticeship laws are being used to advantage. Tourism becomes more important every year; everywhere facilities for visitors are being improved, and this "industry" will doubtless be a growing resource of all Caribbean areas. Britain continues to make substantial grants to the island, Canada has provided a $10 million technical assistance loan, and the United States signed an agreement on February 25, 1959, to make available additional technical aid.

The University College of the West Indies, affiliated with the University of London, was established in 1948 to make it possible to get a higher education without leaving the British Caribbean. The Caribbean Federation has now taken over its operation; it emphasizes quality, and is one of the most effective means yet taken to encourage the British territories to think regionally.

The European areas in the Caribbean, then, also participate in the ferment affecting Latin America. Significant economic, educational, political, and social changes are all under way—but under the discreet guidance of European powers.

— 3 —

COLOMBIA

"Forty Years of Democratic Progress." When the left-wing political leader Jorge Eliécer Gaitán was assassinated in Bogotá on April 9, 1948, Colombians and the world generally could hardly believe what they read in the newspapers. The fact that the ninth Inter-American

Conference was in session there, with General Marshall
leading the U.S. delegation, meant that the story of the
nation-wide outbreak of rioting and looting was carried
to the world in all its dreadful detail. Indiscriminate destruction and looting became general, particularly in the
heart of Bogotá where howling mobs broke into liquor
and hardware stores and raced through the streets armed
with dynamite, machetes, torches, and gasoline. Immense
physical damage was wrought and some 1,200 persons
were killed. Severe damage was also done to the social
fabric of the nation and to the widely held idea that
Colombia represented Latin American democracy at its
best—a cultivated country that produced poets and philologists of distinction, whose National Library was a
model, whose journalists were true men of letters, whose
man on the street in Bogotá spoke the purest Castilian in
the continent, perhaps better Spanish than his counterpart
in Madrid.

The immediate reaction in Colombia and elsewhere
that the 1948 uprising was wholly the work of the Communists has given way slowly to the view that the party
did indeed take advantage of a disturbed situation, but
that basically the bloody events constituted a true social
revolution, not a palace revolt in the time-honored Latin
American pattern. It was eventually recognized that during the previous so-called "forty years of democratic progress" popular democracy had in fact failed to come into
existence and was largely a myth, with power in the hands
of an oligarchy of wealth and of Great Families, an
upper class described as "white, privileged, and competent." (*See Reading No. 25.*) When General Gustavo
Rojas Pinilla seized power from the Conservative President Laureano Gómez in June, 1953, a further blow to
Colombian pride was struck, for dictatorships in Colombia
have been infrequent, unpopular, and brief. The General
was toppled from power only after four years of rule.
During these tumultuous years anti-Protestant activity intensified, and the country entered a period of civil war.
Gravest of all indications of the weakening of the ties
of society in Colombia was the death after 1948 of an
estimated 100,000 people in the undeclared guerrilla wars
which flared up in some parts of the republic between
the Liberals and Conservatives, with bandit elements tak-

ing their toll in the general uproar. What was wrong with the nation?

Inasmuch as Colombia has a highly-educated minority —Bogotá has been called the "Athens of South America" —much attention has been given during recent years to answering this question. In trying to understand the desperate times Colombia has experienced, many writers and foreign observers have emphasized her difficult geography, her one-crop economy, the individualism of Colombians, and the gulf between the powerful, educated minority and the mass of the poor. These writers also suggest that historians have drawn a false picture of Colombia; that they have seen mostly the visible America and not the invisible masses so graphically described by Germán Arciniegas, one of Colombia's most gifted writers. (*See Reading No. 1.*)

Geography, Crops, and Transportation. Even in a continent famous for its physical contrasts, Colombia stands out as unique. Near the equator, its rugged, broken topography has an extraordinary diversity of climates, vegetation, and agricultural crops. Here in juxtaposition are desert wastes, rain forests, temperate valleys, wind-swept barren plains, and snowy peaks. The Chocó area in northwest Colombia, through which the Pan American highway must be built to join with the Panama stretch, consists of thousands of square miles of nearly impenetrable jungle. This unknown land is reported to have 100 mountains more than 8,000 feet high. Down their slopes run some 200 torrential rivers that rise and drop 5 or 6 feet in a few hours, night after night. In eastern Colombia the warm and wet piedmont plains stretch unbroken toward the Orinoco and Amazon rivers. One of Colombia's best-known novels, *La Vorágine* by José Eustacio Rivera, is laid in this Amazonian region. These lowlands occupy more than two-thirds of Colombia's 440,000 square miles but contain less than 2 per cent of its 12 million people.

The Andean highland zone is the Colombia that counts, the Colombia where 6 million bags of coffee are grown annually to account for one-fifth of the world's coffee production and 80 per cent of Colombia's foreign revenue, the Colombia of hillside farms, of oil and orchids, of textile mills and cities. Here live 78 per cent of the

country's population, and here are the three largest cities
—Bogotá (elevation 8,700 feet), Medellín (5,100 feet),
and Cali (3,300 feet).

With the opening of the railroad from the Magdalena
River to Medellín in the 1880's, the volcanic slopes of
Antioquia began to produce for world markets the famous
mild Colombian coffee. The proud and frugal "Antioqueños," with their aggressive colonizing genius and high
birth rate—families of 15 and 20 are not uncommon even
today in upper class as well as poor families—have been
the most important single force behind the economic
growth and development of the country since 1900. Their
family-size farms produce more than three-fourths of Colombia's coffee crop. Medellín is today a bustling city of
half a million people; many of the largest banks, industries, and transportation companies are located there and
many a modern capitalist started penniless there. The
Antioqueños through initiative and hard work have produced a relatively democratic society based upon industry
and upon many small landholdings.

Another important region is the Cauca valley, in
southwestern Colombia, an extraordinarily attractive area
which once held great cattle and sugar estates but is
gradually diversifying its agriculture as the floods that
plague it are brought under control. The ambitious Cauca
Valley Development project, a 20-year plan modeled on
TVA, includes power, flood control, irrigation, reclama-
tion, reforestation, and mineral and industrial development.

Colombian transport was mainly limited to river navi-
gation for more than three centuries following the Spanish
conquest. The lower Magdalena, navigable for 615 miles
from its mouth on the Caribbean to the rapids at La
Dorada, has been the lifeline linking the interior with the
coast and the outside world. From various river ports,
railroads, aerial cables, and truck roads have been built
to the principal highland centers. The trip from the coast
to Bogotá still requires five to seven days on a river boat,
depending on the season, and another day by rail or road.
This situation will be greatly improved when the new
railroad running from Barranquilla on the Caribbean
along the Magdalena River to La Dorada is completed.

The new Paz del Río blast furnace and steel mill (capacity 122,000 tons) dramatically illustrates Colombia's basic transportation problem. Built in isolated highlands at an elevation of almost 9,000 feet, 150 miles north of Bogotá and even farther from other large consuming centers, it is ideally located for raw materials, since iron ore, coal, and limestone are in ample supply nearby. But Paz del Río steel delivered in Colombia is sometimes more costly than imported steel because of transportation and manufacturing costs. Only a high protective tariff, at the expense of the Colombian consumer, can make the project "economic." Yet it has a symbolic role in Colombia, eager to demonstrate its maturity by industrialization. "For those who believe that a national steel industry is justifiable at any price, Paz del Río is indeed a new El Dorado; for others, perhaps, the ailing steel mill . . . is a grotesque and costly monument to misguided nationalism." [10]

Colombia was the first country in the Americas to establish a regular air service when Scadta was inaugurated in 1919 with German pilots and capital. It quickly expanded its service throughout the country and to adjacent countries. In 1940 it merged with a Pan-American Airways subsidiary to form Avianca which held a monopoly until the end of the war when numerous competitive companies began to flourish. Much cargo that would move by land in other countries goes by air in Colombia; ironically her superior air service has delayed the development of an adequate overland transport system. The one-hour flight between Bogotá and Medellín costs little more than the 24-hour truck trip over a tortuous mountain road.

Air service meant political as well as economic changes. Provincial barriers crumbled, or seemed to, the press found a national audience, and for the first time political and social integration appeared possible.

The Colombian People.   The conquistadores virtually annihilated the warlike Indians along the Caribbean coast, and found it necessary to import slaves from Senegal and the Congo in the seventeenth and eighteenth centuries. Cartagena became a Negro center, made noteworthy by the Jesuit Alonso de Sandoval's advocacy of Christian treatment for the Negro slaves and for his pro-

[10] C. Langdon White and Donald J. Alderson, "Steel and Symbolism at Paz del Río," *Inter-American Economic Affairs,* IX (Spring, 1956), pp. 92-94.

posal, about 1650, that a School of African Studies be set up to forward the work of the missionaries. One of his disciples was another Jesuit, Pedro Claver, Colombia's only saint. Today the descendants of the slaves constitute a small percentage of the population and are to be found concentrated in the hot coastal areas. About half the population of Colombia have mixed Indian-Spanish blood, about one-quarter are white, and the balance are mulattoes. In attempting to characterize the Colombians, most observers, native and foreign, emphasize the strong influence of the wide geographical differences already described. Psychological traits have developed in the various regions: "The Antioqueño is traditionalist, regionalist, conquering, intrepid, and neurotic. . . . The Nariñense is sober, highly industrious and hospitable, passionate in his religious and political beliefs, obstinate to excess. . . . The Costeño is expansive, conceited, and vehement." [11]

The temper of the politically conscious minority has been described as "anarchistic," deriving from its Hispanic inheritance, and "every Colombian is a political party." (*See Reading No. 26.*) Simón Bolívar, the revolutionary hero of Colombia, declared that, "To form a stable government, one must have as a national base a general spirit whose object is to incline everyone uniformly toward two points: moderation of the general will, and limitation of public authority." It is doubtful that such a spirit has ever existed in Colombia.

Luis López de Mesa, one of Colombia's brilliant intellects, developed the idea that Colombia represented the true synthesis of all Latin America. This dream was rudely interrupted by the turmoil and trouble of Colombia's postwar years.

"The Salutary Change." For almost a century after 1810, when Bogotá banished the Viceroy and proclaimed the Act of Independence, Colombia suffered a long period of intermittent anarchy. She experienced ten revolutions of national scope, some seventy more limited uprisings, and in 1900-1902 a bloody civil conflict called "The War of the Thousand Days," in which the country's

[11] Juvenal Mejía Córdoba, as quoted by W. O. Galbraith, *Colombia. A General Survey,* London: Royal Institute of International Affairs, 1953, p. 23.

economy was gravely damaged and some 100,000 men
are said to have perished.

The twentieth century brought spectacular changes beginning with the loss of Panama in 1903, which embit-
tered Colombian-U.S. relations for a generation. The
Conservative Party assumed control of the country and
kept it until 1930. Meanwhile World War I brought the
impact of at least temporary new markets and, following
the Russian Revolution of 1917, the old social balance
was disturbed by the spread of proletarian doctrines which
in turn led to the growth of militant labor unionism. Foreign money poured into Colombia during the 1920's. The
$25,000,000 of U.S. "conscience money" paid to heal the
breach over Panama was devoted to the building of ports,
highways, and railroads. Foreign oil companies invested
some $45,000,000. A veritable tidal wave of $200,000,000
was loaned by U.S. bankers to the Colombian government, departments, and municipalities for an expansion
of coffee production, development of textile industries,
and other improvements. Corruption and inflation came
in its wake.

When the worldwide depression of 1929 reached Colombia in the form of low coffee prices, the Conservatives
were discredited and their split made it possible for the
Liberals to come into office peacefully after half a
century of Conservative domination. Alfonso López, a
wealthy patrician, served as Liberal President 1934-1938,
and worked for a reform program that included land
laws, improvement of the status and conditions of workers, recognition that public assistance is a function of the
state, and a firmly imposed progressive tax on income
and utilities. For the first time in Colombian history,
government income no longer depended primarily on customs revenues, and a potent source of political graft was
thereby eliminated.

The moderate wing of the Liberals installed Eduardo
Santos as President 1938-1942, and the reform movement
began to slacken. Santos owned and edited the powerful
El Tiempo, one of the outstanding newspapers in the
Americas, and gave his strong support to the United
States in World War II. When López re-won the presi-
dency 1942-1946, he carried on Santos' policy both of

support for the allies and of no reform. His ministers
were often millionaires; the war years brought charges
of corruption and even unsavory scandals touching the
President's own family. After a series of unpleasant in-
cidents, one of which was his capture for several days
by Army elements in a provincial capital, López stepped
down in August, 1945, and Alberto Lleras Camargo was
brought back from the Colombian Embassy in Washington with bipartisan support to serve out the last year of
the presidential term as a holding operation.

The Conservatives regained power in 1946, when the
veteran Conservative Laureano Gómez selected Mariano
Ospina Pérez as his party's candidate, and won against
a divided Liberal Party which had put up two candidates,
one of whom, Jorge Eliécer Gaitán, stood for reforms for
the benefit of the masses.

Colombia went steadily downhill under President Ospina. Inflation increased rapidly under the abnormal economic situation in the wake of the war, black marketeer-
ing became standard practice, and the cost of living for
the masses rose sharply but not their income. The murder
of Gaitán in 1948 sparked off an orgy of rioting that was
the product of an unstable political and social situation
of long standing. When Laureano Gómez returned from
Spain in 1948 to run for president, the gulf between the
two parties became impassable. He won the election by
a vote of 1,140,619 against 15, the Liberals abstaining
from the polls. Some well-to-do Liberals welcomed his
victory, for they were tired of instability and felt that a
businesslike strong man like Gómez "might be a salutary
change."

**Background for the Dictatorship of General Gustavo
Rojas Pinilla.** Gómez as President brought prosperity
to the upper classes, thanks to higher coffee prices and
freedom from wartime economic controls. Exports almost
doubled during 1949-1953, labor organization was discouraged, and the index of living rose steeply. As he began to rule personally and autocratically, opposition began
to form; even some members of his Conservative Party
declared against his authoritarian rule. Gómez sent Colombian troops to Korea, in cooperation with the United
Nations, an action that was viewed as an attempted diver-
sion from national troubles and as a way of transferring

army control from the Liberals to the Conservatives. Liberals were considered "bandits" and hunted down mercilessly; two Liberal newspapers were burned and the rest controlled. Many of Gómez' followers were alienated by his proposed constitutional changes which would give the Catholic Church greater political and temporal power, and set up a corporate fascist-like system of government. The army at last stepped in on June 15, 1953, Gómez fled, and General Rojas Pinilla's bloodless coup was hailed by a weary country close to exhaustion after years of uncertainty and violence. His popularity faded when he restored press censorship, incurred the enmity of the Church, and attempted to create a third party that would replace Conservative and Liberals.

His four-year rule did not pacify Colombia; he found he could accomplish little of the social reform he promised. Guerrilla warfare over political differences continued throughout the land along with plain banditry; in addition, the dictator and high Catholic officials charged that Protestants were Communists or Communist fronts. The countryside was kept in an uproar by the religious, political, and economic hostilities that divided the nation. With both parties united against him, Rojas Pinilla intensified the state of siege he had ordered on coming into power. In desperation the Conservatives and Liberals joined hands to force him into exile on May 10, 1957. In January, 1959, he returned voluntarily to stand trial in Bogotá before the Senate; one of the charges was that he and his wife had illegally enriched themselves by millions of dollars; in March he was found guilty, by an overwhelming vote, of violating the constitution and of injuring the dignity of the presidency.

Rojas Pinilla's place in Colombian history will long be debated. He put into motion some economic projects recommended by the Currie Mission sent by the International Bank, inaugurated the Paz del Río steel mill, and pushed the Cauca Valley "TVA" project. Probably no government could have achieved much in a country so deeply disturbed; both parties were internally divided. One writer described the situation in these terms: "the vast majority of the voters are either illiterate or totally uneducated, and the social system itself is unstable; the masses are subject to emotional, impractical, and self-

interested propaganda, and now that they have learned
their strength and tasted blood, it is going to be a hard
task for any government to correct and control the political errors and exaggerations of the last thirty years." [12]

Bipartisan Government. Two ex-presidents, the
Conservative Laureano Gómez and the Liberal Alberto
Lleras Camargo, meeting in the Spanish seaport Sitges,
issued on July 20, 1957, a unique and notable agreement
which aimed to bring political peace to their nation by
proposing a bipartisan government for a period of twelve
years. (*See Reading No. 27.*) This historic moment
brought together two of the most powerful and diverse
figures in Colombian political annals. Gómez was trained
as an engineer but early embarked on a political career
in Congress in which his invective and polemical power
was given free rein. In 1938, for example, he denounced
mild and scholarly President Santos as a "murderer . . .
who sits in pools of Conservative blood." In the 1948-
1953 era he tried to force on Colombia a ruthless dictatorship modeled after that of Franco in Spain, whom he
admired. A thoroughgoing aristocrat, he represents a
feudalistic landed gentry and believes that the Catholic
Church must be, after government, the main force in society. Lleras Camargo entered journalism as a youth and
by his middle-twenties had achieved distinction as a
writer; he was a Cabinet Minister at 29, Ambassador to
Washington at 37, in 1945-1946 served as President when
López left, and from 1948 to 1952 was the first Latin
American to hold the office of Secretary General of the
Organization of American States. He is not a Strong Man,
but a wise one who since 1945 has believed that "National Union," a coalition of the two parties, is the only
way to save Colombia. The joint "Declaration of Beni-
dorm" of these two men had in 1956 paved the way for
a successful attack on Dictator Rojas Pinilla; the Pact of
Sitges was a natural step in 1957. The agreement made
there to put the Congress, Cabinet, and Presidency under
bipartisan auspices for twelve years was ratified in Colombia, later extended to a sixteen-year period, and led
to the election of Lleras Camargo and his inauguration
as President in August, 1958. Will the truce endure? And
[12] Galbraith, *Colombia,* p. 135.

if it does, will the period of political peace be utilized to undertake the fundamental economic and social reforms so urgently required?

"The Most Urgent Need of Colombia." Lleras Camargo, who twice risked the future of the Liberal Party and his own political fortunes by joining with the controversial Conservative Gómez, appears to understand the gravity of the situation, for he wrote in 1955: "The most urgent necessity of Colombia is that of preparing a numerous group of people with the capacity to manage and resolve the elemental problems of a collective type of life which is spreading over the planet with tremendous rapidity. This type of life is the consequence of the great industrial revolution which enlarged and made more dangerous the distance between the rich and the poor people. . . . The new problems are . . . more general, because they concern human beings; masses, with a very definite consciousness of their rights." [13]

This "collective type of life" implies a change of outlook for the upper classes of Colombia and for the small middle class group which has usually sided with them. As the French Dominican Louis Lebret stated in a report made to the dictator Rojas Pinilla, but suppressed by him: "The primary Colombian problem is a social one, of irrational political quarrels in the face of realities obscured by poor statistics. There is a lack of directive courage capable of furnishing scientific leadership to the country. The leaders are not aware of Colombian social realities within the world scene, and consider any national progress in terms of an increase in their personal fortunes. The standard of living of the middle and working classes has declined, while financial inflation continues, and popular education is devoid of practical meaning and efficacy. The difference between the standard of living of the wealthy (5%) and that of the other economic classes in Colombia is greater than in more highly developed countries." [14]

[13] As quoted by Vernon Lee Fluharty, *Dance of the Millions,* Pittsburgh: University of Pittsburgh Press, 1957, pp. 149-150.

[14] As given by *Hispanic American Report,* X (Stanford University, 1957), pp. 479-480.

Lebret went on to recommend various agricultural and other policies to avert the ruin that he predicted unless drastic reforms were made.

Another flood of light on Colombia's urgent needs has been shed by Orlando Fals-Borda, one of the few Colombian sociologists who has analyzed social facts and problems by direct observation and measurement of social phenomena in the field, instead of relying on theoretical statements. His study of a small rural community near Bogotá combines statistical facts and generalizations of remarkable insight.[15] The fact that he has been named Chairman of the newly established Department of Sociology at the University of Colombia and appointed in January, 1959, Director General of the Department of Agriculture "to put into effect a much needed reform in agriculture" indicates that his ideas have won favor in the Lleras Camargo government. He concludes that the "rural people of Colombia are being swept into the whirl of social revolution that promises to be the distinguishing feature of our century. . . . As yet no clear-cut crisis has arisen in Colombian rural areas as a result of this historical transition, but there is unrest. This is not the same political unrest that attracted the attention of the world to Colombia during the last five years. It is, rather, an unprecedented feeling of dissatisfaction penetrating the masses of Colombia's farmers and laborers; it is an awakening due to an increasing class consciousness." [16]

This Colombian sociologist and government official knows the depth of poverty in the country, that the number of illiterates actually increased from 3¼ to 4 million during the period 1937 to 1947, and that the majority of the people live in houses of adobe or bamboo with earthen floors and straw-thatched roofs, and lack a water supply and sewage system. But do those who make the ultimate political decisions understand the implications of these facts? The Pact of Sitges was a political document that made no reference to economic or social affairs. If the peace sought by Gómez and Lleras Camargo at Sitges

---

[15] *Peasant Society in the Colombian Andes. A Sociological Study of Saucío,* Gainesville: University of Florida Press, 195.

[16] *Ibid.,* p. vii.

results merely in the union of what have been described as "the two conservative parties," the future of Colombia may be as stormy as her past fifteen years.

The words of Mordecai to Esther, which Dr. Fals-Borda sets at the beginning of his volume, indicate the urgency with which he and other Colombians aware of the social realities of their country view the task before the bipartisan government now in power: "Think not that in the king's palace you will escape . . . For if you keep silence at such a time as this, relief and deliverance will rise . . . from another quarter. . . . Who knows whether you have not come for such a time as this?"

— 4 —

VENEZUELA

Bolívar, Dictators, and Oil. When Rómulo Betancourt became President of Venezuela on February 12, 1959, he assumed the leadership of a country whose history has been linked to that of her neighbor Colombia by the Liberator Simón Bolívar, who freed both nations from Spain during the tumultuous revolutionary period 1810-1830. Otherwise the countries have little in common and have relatively little to do with each other in spite of their physical proximity. Venezuela's 6 million people are largely mestizos and thus much more homogeneous than Colombia's population, and Venezuela has no Church-State problem. After 1860 a strong anti-clerical movement reduced the privileges of the Church step by step; its financial independence was destroyed, its social leadership abolished, and in the end it became a relatively unimportant force in public and social life.

Venezuela furnished many of the soldiers who followed Bolívar on his triumphant sweep through the lands now

known as Colombia, Ecuador, Peru, and even as far south
as the mining center Potosí in Bolivia. On the summit of
this mountain some 15,000 feet above sea level with the
flags of the newly liberated nations fluttering in the breeze,
the Liberator declaimed in 1825: "We come victorious
from the Atlantic coast. In fifteen years of continuous
and terrific strife, we have destroyed the edifice that tyranny erected during three centuries of usurpation and
uninterrupted violence. . . . Standing here on this silver
mountain of Potosí, whose rich veins were Spain's treasury for three hundred years, I must declare my belief
that this material wealth is as nothing compared with the
glory of bearing the ensign of freedom from the shores
of the Orinoco to plant it on the summit of a mountain
which is the admiration and envy of the world." This
glamorous tradition of glory Bolívar bequeathed to his
native land, Venezuela, which still feels the influence of
Bolívar and is moved by his memory.

Another result of the revolution was the heavy loss of
life and property, for in Venezuela Spaniards and revo-
lutionists fought the "War to the Death." One-quarter of
the population is estimated to have died, including a large
proportion of her young men. The economic confusion
following independence and the political inexperience of
her people help to explain the succeeding anarchy and
despotism. Venezuela became notorious for her dictators
in a continent where they flourished, and the purple prose
used to flatter them became famous. (*See Reading No.
29.*)

  "Democratic Caesarism." The variety of Venezuelan dictators is impressive. José Antonio Páez, the cowboy
revolutionary leader who opposed Bolívar's grandiose
schemes outside of Venezuela, served as a conservative
dictator (1830-1846, 1861-1863). While in exile in New
York City he wrote his memoirs. Antonio Guzmán
Blanco was an educated gentleman familiar with European capitals, a strong foe of the Church, and most famous for the centralized corruption he imposed during
his eighteen-year rule (1870-1888). His vanity was colossal, for he delighted in and insisted upon his lackeys
referring to him as "Illustrious American" or "National
Regenerator," and even more bombastic titles. He loved
music, built an imposing opera house in Caracas, and

during his last years became a sybaritic waster in Paris.

Cipriano Castro (1899-1908) was the most dissolute and one of the most corrupt, and provoked a blockade by European naval units in 1902. Juan Antonio Gómez, the trusted lieutenant of Castro who succeeded him in 1908, proved one of the most savage of all. A hard-working abstemious dictator, he drank little, was not interested in titles, and stayed in Venezuela attending to his business. He became the richest man in South America with his hand in almost every economic enterprise in Venezuela, particularly oil. He maintained good relations with foreign powers, improved sanitation, and even built a few schools. His rule was called "Democratic Caesarism" by those who accepted it as the only way to avoid chaos and anarchy. Gil Fortoul, one of Venezuela's outstanding historians, saw no contradiction or betrayal of principles in serving the great dictator for many years as political advisor at home and as diplomat abroad. In his eyes, only a "strong and good man" could give Venezuela what she needed most: peace, progress, and order. Gómez gave Venezuela peace, but the price was an army of spies and jails full of political prisoners who often suffered severe tortures. When "The Well-Deserving" died in 1935, Venezuelans rioted in the streets and fired the homes of his numerous sons and henchmen.

Movement Toward Democracy, 1935-1959. Venezuela was not prepared for the problems of undictatorial government, and for ten years semi-dictatorial regimes prevailed. General Isaías Medina Angarita (1941-1945) supported the United States in World War II, permitted opposition parties to exist, the largest of which was Acción Democrática, and in general governed moderately. The army seized control in November, 1945, and Acción Democrática under the leadership of Rómulo Betancourt won the Congressional elections of 1946, and then elected the famous novelist Rómulo Gallegos as President. Acción Democrática, made up of civilians, labor leaders, middle-class professionals and businessmen, incorporated the party's principles in a new constitution embodying social legislation which included the nation's right to expropriate oil properties and to elect the president by direct popular vote. Gallegos began his term of office in February, 1948, but remained only ten months. Apparently he tried to go too fast too soon, and alienated important army officers, landowners, and businessmen. Gallegos and Betancourt were exiled; the brief experiment in democracy was over.

A military junta now exercised dictatorial power. Acción Democrática went underground, the junta jailed opponents freely and used tear gas against demonstrating university students. The junta arranged for an election in November, 1952, but when unexpected opposition strength threatened, the dominant member of the junta, General Marcos Pérez Jiménez, simply announced that he had won by an overwhelming majority, and Venezuela was back again under a one-man dictatorship.

The Pérez Jiménez regime was a tough autocracy which insisted that the economic development of the nation was supreme, and that to bring traditional democracy would only precipitate chaos and interfere with the material progress of Venezuela. As the Interior Minister Dr. Laureano Vallenilla Lanz stated the case, in words reminiscent of "Democratic Caesarism": "It is absurd to attempt to build a democracy in a backward, uneducated nation." The Acción Democrática leaders in exile accused the dictator of wasting the national wealth in spectacular but unproductive public works, and the Archbishop of Caracas, Mons. Rafael Arias Blanco, on May 1, 1957, wrote in his pastoral letter that "nobody will dare affirm that wealth is distributed in a manner that reaches all the Venezuelans, since an immense mass of our people are living in conditions that cannot be designated as human."

Another facet of the social situation is the instability of the Venezuelan home. "Marriage has never been a popular institution in Venezuela. . . . In terms of cold statistics, 51.9 per cent of the children born in the country in 1949 were illegitimate; 7 per cent, though illegitimate, were recognized by their fathers, which presumably guaranteed some support; only 41.1 per cent, the products of legal marriages, would know the security of a normal family relationship. What is more, some women —saddled with children they cannot feed—follow the example of the men. According to the Consejo del Niño, a branch of the Venezuelan Department of Justice, there are about 90,000 abandoned children in the country. That is roughly 2 per cent of Venezuela's total population." [17]

The Pérez Jiménez dictatorship remained in power through the support of the military establishment—whose clubs and other facilities made possible by oil revenues reached extraordinary heights of luxury—and through the chillingly efficient secret police. But all dictators fall at last. On January 23, 1958, dissident Navy and Air Force units made possible the courageous and unanimous action—by practically all elements of society in Venezuela, from labor unions to lawyers, from people living in the miserable "ranchos" in the hills overlooking Caracas to substantial businessmen—which overthrew Pérez Jiménez.

An immense feeling of freedom swept over the country, mixed with a certain indignation against the United States, which partially explains the rough treatment accorded Vice-President Nixon during his visit in May, 1958. Venezuelans had resented the friendly U.S. gestures made to Pérez Jiménez during the height of his oppressive rule, such as the medal given the dictator, the gala reception in Washington for his dreaded police chief Pedro Estrada, the close personal relations between one U.S. ambassador and the dictator, and the fact that Pérez Jiménez was allowed to take up luxurious residence in Miami after the people had ejected him from Venezuela. After the Nixon incident, reports in U.S. newspapers and magazines that carried what Venezuelans considered greatly exaggerated estimates of Communist influence in their country deepened Venezuelan displeasure and aroused a storm of anti-U.S. feeling. The charge was heard in Caracas—and was given currency by the Communists themselves—that the United States was planning to inflate "the Communist menace" in order to justify action in Venezuela as in the case of Guatemala.

The veteran Acción Democrática leader Rómulo Betancourt won the presidential election in 1959, and on February 12 was inaugurated amid general rejoicing. Important issues faced the new government. Will the military permit the President to rule, and how will Venezuela's long-range relationships with the foreign business inter-

[17] William D. and Amy L. Marsland, *Venezuela Through Its History*, New York: Thomas Y. Crowell Co., 1954, p. 262.

ests be conducted? Although the new government inherited a debt from the dictator of $1.5 billion, Venezuela's leading bankers, businessmen, and economists manifest cautious optimism about the future. They share President Betancourt's conviction, expressed in his declaration made in 1956 in exile, that the Venezuelan people and the country are essentially sound. (*See Reading No. 31.*)

One of the most powerful reasons for Venezuelan optimism is the existence of oil, which deeply colors the country's economic and political life today. No city in the Americas, with the possible exception of São Paulo in Brazil, has been so dramatically transformed during the last twenty-five years as Caracas. Once a delightful town with a certain colonial air lingering on, Caracas now has built a sort of Rockefeller Center downtown; four-lane super-highways are available for the many automobiles, which choke the older, narrow streets; luxurious hotels attract cosmopolitan guests, and life proceeds at a dizzy —and expensive—pace. Well-to-do Venezuelans find vacations in New York inexpensive, set up foundations for various purposes, and have supplanted Argentines as free-spenders abroad. All this has resulted from oil, whose power now rivals that of the political dictators.

The New Dictator.   Venezuelans have always been primarily farmers, and three-quarters of the population today live off the land. Most of these wring a precarious living out of the steep slopes of the Andes on which in other countries farming would not be attempted. Cultivation methods are often primitive and wasteful, which helps to explain the yield of only two bushels of corn to the acre, as compared with 40 bushels in central United States. The average Venezuelan, therefore, is accustomed to austerity; his food intake has been estimated at about one quarter of that required by a European immigrant.

Some good agricultural lands are found in the Maracaibo lowlands, but the rest of Venezuela is disappointing to the farmer. The southernmost region, the Guayana Hinterland, is relatively inaccessible, little exploited, and in parts unexplored. The sandstone mountains, which inspired Sir Arthur Conan Doyle to write *The Lost World,* still await ambitious ornithologists, botanists, and other scientists to unravel their mysteries. Gold and diamonds are found in this vast region, but the greatest potential is in the rich iron deposits on its northern edge.

North of Guayana are the thinly settled plains (*Llanos*) or grasslands which produced General Páez and his cowboy fighters who helped Bolívar win Venezuelan independence from the trained Spanish soldiers. The llanos are subject to serious floods in the rainy season, and under the hot sun of the dry season their clay soils become hardpan. It was on or near these plains that T. S. Stribling located the story of that literary but credible dictator *Fombombo* (1923). Agricultural development has taken place in Venezuela, but the solemn and limiting fact is that much of the land is difficult to cultivate or poor—hence the spectacular importance of oil in Venezuela's economy.

When the Spaniards arrived at Maracaibo in 1499 they found the Indians using oil for medicine and other purposes, but it was never commercially significant until the twentieth century. The nineteenth century, however, saw important laws passed on oil extraction. Subsoil deposits were made the property of the nation, not the surface owner, and the authority to grant oil leases was exclusively reserved for the President. As the world began to use oil, British, Dutch, and American companies moved into Venezuela, but the industry lagged until 1919. Dictator Gómez encouraged exploration by the 1922 basic oil law which Edwin Lieuwen has called a "liberal, clear, simple, workable statute," though royalties of only 7½ to 10 per cent were paid.[18] Gómez, however, had a whole bag full of tricks which enabled him personally to secure a considerable slice of the profits. The years 1923-1929 were boom years when Venezuela rose from an insignificant producer to become second only to the United States among the world's petroleum producing nations. In Maracaibo, the hottest city in South America and the center of the nation's oil industry, living costs doubled and real-estate values tripled. By 1930 Gómez had completed paying off the entire foreign debt, with oil revenues. When he died in 1935, "an economic dictator had already inherited Venezuela . . . the petroleum industry was the new ruler. The new tyrant was immortal, and political upheavals disturbed it little. It answered only to the demands of the market in the United States and in western Europe

[18] Edwin Lieuwen, *Petroleum in Venezuela. A History*, Berkeley: University of California Press, 1954, p. 27.

and waited for the signals to be called from abroad." [19]

The Great Debate. At the death of Gómez, Venezuelans began to debate whether petroleum was a blessing or a curse to the country, and this argument continues. Those who take the affirmative side stress that the great oil development cost the government nothing, for the foreign companies built roads, mapped large areas, paid Venezuelans high wages, and improved their living conditions generally. (*See Reading No. 28.*) They emphasize that taxes provide the chief source of revenue for the government.

The critics assert that the large profits made by the foreign companies had an unsettling effect on the nation's economy, that oil helped to keep corrupt dictators in power and hindered a real attack on such problems as education, health, and agriculture. Oil provides a slippery base for a nation's economy, they conclude, and insist that Venezuela is now dangerously dependent on a single foreign-owned industry which fluctuates violently due to the uncertain demands of a capricious world market.

One result of this debate was that, after Gómez, both military dictators and popularly elected presidents have energetically and persistently worked to increase Venezuela's share in oil profits. General Medina's basic 1943 law unified petroleum legislation and, in return for certain concessions to the oil companies, provided that total taxes and royalties should ultimately assure Venezuela 50 per cent of the profits—a revolutionary concept at the time which was specifically written into the law of 1948. What the post-Gómez governments have done with these profits is a much disputed story. Each successive government has proclaimed the policy of "sowing the petroleum," of ploughing the oil profits back into the soil of the nation in the form of roads, hospitals, and other public works. Roads have indeed been built, though sometimes an ultra-modern expressway passes through towns that have as yet no water, sewers, telephones, or medical facilities. A splendid new University of Caracas, an Officers' Club that offers the last word in comfort and elegance, a University hospital with more than 1,100 beds, and low-cost family housing are also products of this policy. More than half of the government funds for

[19] *Ibid.,* p. 71.

public works have been spent in or near the capital, Caracas, and one foreign observer has concluded that up to 1954 the policy had failed to benefit the country as a whole and that responsibility for this rests largely upon the Army. (*See Reading No. 30.*)

When President Betancourt took office in February, 1959, the oil companies feared higher taxes and they were right. Nationalization of the industry is not involved, but a 60 per cent share for Venezuela is now contemplated. Meanwhile oil production continues at about 3 million barrels a day, despite the familiar cry of "Keep out foreign oil" heard in the U.S. Congress and the fact that only 3 per cent of the labor force of Venezuela extract the petroleum which accounts for over 90 per cent of Venezuela's foreign income and provides 63 per cent of her government revenues. The size of this "economic tyrant" may be seen from the fact that one American company alone, Creole, has produced in Venezuela in recent years approximately half as much oil as the U.S.S.R., the world's third largest producing country. But even this powerful industry may be challenged in the future when the huge iron deposits south of the Orinoco River are fully exploited. Bethlehem Steel started operations in 1951; United States Steel, which discovered a mountain, Cerro Bolívar, containing an estimated half billion tons of high-grade ore, invested $50 million in a railroad and other facilities, and began to move ore out in 1954.

The Future. If President Betancourt's goverment can weather political storms and come to a satisfactory relationship with the oil companies, the resulting peace will afford Venezuela her first sustained opportunity to grapple with her basic problems. If the government "sows" her petroleum and iron profits wisely, the harvest produced will eventually raise the standard of living of the Venezuelan people.

5

MEXICO

Mexico as Seen from Chapultepec Hill. For centuries the finest view of Mexico City has been one from this wooded eminence which first appeared in history as an Aztec fortification. In 1521 the conquistador Ferdinand Cortez gazed from Chapultepec out upon the island-city of Tenochtitlán, then the home of perhaps 30,000 Indians ruled by Montezuma. In the eighteenth century the Spanish viceroys who enjoyed Chapultepec as a summer residence saw a colonial capital of 100,000 Spaniards, Indians, and mestizos. When General Winfield Scott stormed the Hill on September 13, 1847, despite the heroic resistance of the boy-cadets, to bring the U.S.-Mexican War to a military close, the population stood at 200,000. As late as 1910, when Porfirio Díaz's dictatorial regime was coming to an end, there were only about 400,000 inhabitants, and Mexico City was still a provincial seat. Today visitors who flock to historic Chapultepec Hill see spread before them a great metropolis of nearly 5 million people, surpassed in size in the Western Hemisphere only by New York, Chicago, Los Angeles, and Buenos Aires. Since the city grows about 5 per cent annually, Mexico City may overtake Moscow by 1960.

The oldest city on the North American continent, it is also becoming one of the most modern. Despite a spongy subsoil which makes construction difficult, Mexico City has now an imposing skyline, dominated by the tallest building (44 stories) in Latin America. Many tall glass-sheathed government and private buildings rise above the dignified tree-lined Paseo de la Reforma that leads from the base of Chapultepec Hill to downtown Mexico City. South of the city are located the dazzling new buildings of the continent's oldest university and the adjacent residential area Pedregal, where modern architecture flourishes. Circling airliners mark the location of the great international air terminal in the east section of the city.

The six-year term of President Adolfo Ruiz Cortines (1953-1958) saw a remarkable construction record. On one single day, in a feverish, end-of-term spurt, the President and Ernesto P. Uruchurtu, federal district governor and the Robert Moses of Mexico, inaugurated 12 public markets, 23 schools, a modern police headquarters, a central fire station, a streetcar and trolley bus terminal, and a model penitentiary which includes a guest house to make possible regular visits of wives of prisoners. The last of the famous downtown street markets, the Lagunilla and the Merced, have been removed to spacious new quarters in which methods in use since Montezuma's time have been abolished; now the vendors occupy sanitary concrete buildings provided with running water and refrigeration.

Descending from the Hill, one begins to see evidence of the strain that such spectacular growth has created. One-third of Mexico City's population live in squalor on the edge of the city or in downtown slums. Shanty suburbs of tin and cardboard testify to the flood of thousands of country-folk choosing to endure miserable living conditions in the capital rather than to remain in rural districts. This flood has swept in so rapidly that the government is hard-put to finance such new and sorely needed public services as water, lights, drainage, paved streets, transportation, and public health facilities. Meanwhile, thousands of the rural poor make their way north, legally or illegally, to the United States in spite of the hard conditions of life they sometimes meet there.

Leaving Mexico City by any of the modern highways that lead away from it, one sees the dramatic running battle between progress and poverty raging—in industrial Monterrey near the Texas border, in Guadalajara to the northwest, in Oaxaca to the south and, indeed, everywhere in this republic of almost 32 million people. It was estimated in 1956 that more than 60 per cent of the population were poorly fed, housed, and clothed, 40 per cent were illiterate, and 40 per cent of the children of school age did not attend school. Though Indians—defined as those who speak one of the 50 distinct native languages and wear traditional clothing—constitute now only about

10 per cent of the population, many of them suffer extreme misery and live much as their ancestors did at the time Montezuma was in power.

Looking at Mexico City from Chapultepec Hill, then, striking contrasts and apparent contradictions are clearly visible. To understand them, one must return to the background of the Revolution.

Pre-Revolutionary Mexico. Ernest Gruening has thus summarized the essential features of the Spanish colonial regime which lasted nearly 300 years after Cortez conquered Tenochtitlán in 1521: "It was a period of comparative peace—the peace of suppression, stagnation, and decay. Its outstanding characteristics were: politically—absentee absolutism resting on military and religious domination, with complete denial of local self-expression and self-training, and disregard by officials of laws that it was to their interest to disregard; economically—extraction or raw materials based on slave labor, with office-holding the universal desideratum; socially—splendor and privilege contrasted with misery and degradation; spiritually—corruption, ignorance, fanaticism, intercaste hatred." Though this view of colonial Mexico is a simplified and not wholly accurate one, many of the revolutionaries both in 1810 and 1910 believed that this was their whole heritage from Spain.

The movement which brought Mexico independence from Spain in 1821 did little to alter the colonial social and economic structure. Not until the framing of the Constitution of 1857 and the subsequent enactment of various laws to restrict the economic and political power of the Church did reform begin. President Benito Juárez, a full-blooded Zapotec Indian, was the great figure during the next decade, but he was too busy fighting Maximilian and the French, between 1862-1867, and entrenched Mexican conservatives to implement the Constitution and the various reform laws. La Reforma ended in November, 1876, when Porfirio Díaz, under the remarkable slogan, "effective suffrage—no re-election," set up his dictatorship which endured, save for a four-year interval, for thirty-four years. The previous half-century had been a period of almost continuous instability; under Díaz the national budget was balanced, national income increased fivefold, Mexico was "prosperous" and could borrow all the money it wanted at about 5 per cent. But the over-whelming majority of Mexicans were poor; 1 per cent of the population owned most of the land, which was worked by landless peasants whose standard of living declined steadily. One economist states that agricultural wages remained constant from 1810 to 1910, but that the cost of food for the agricultural workers increased 300 per cent.

The relation of the peons to the upperclass landowners was generally one of complete dependence. The typical hacienda included homes of workers, the hacienda store where they had to buy their supplies at high prices which led them into debt slavery, a chapel, a jail, a cemetery, and, sometimes, a school. The owner ordinarily lived in Mexico City or a provincial capital, and left the hacienda to be directed by a mayordomo who rode his territory with a gun or whip in hand to stimulate recalcitrant workers and protect himself from attack.

Díaz and his clique organized Mexico into one vast machine whose monopoly of political power was main-tained by its monopoly of police power, the *rurales* (rural police), and the army. The Church generally preached submission to authority, whether dictator, hacendado, factory owner, or mine superintendent. The pastoral letter of the Archbishop Francisco Orozco y Jiménez of Guada-lajara has been cited as typical of this viewpoint, although the message was promulgated in Revolutionary days: "As all authority is derived from God, the Christian workman should sanctify and make sublime his obedience by serv-ing God in the person of his bosses. In this way obedience is neither humiliating nor difficult. . . . Poor, love your humble state and your work; turn your gaze towards Heaven; there is the true wealth." [20]

Indians were considered "racially inferior" and lazy; when the Indians opposed the robbery by hacendados of the land they had held for centuries, they were mercilessly repressed. Between 1883 and 1894, Díaz and his obedient Congress gave away to foreign speculators and personal friends one-fifth of the entire area of the Republic, or 134,500,000 acres of the public domain. By 1910 less than 10 per cent of the Indian communities had any land whatever, and the Indians themselves were social outcasts

[20] As quoted by Clarence Senior, *Land Reform and Democracy,* Gainesville: University of Florida Press, 1958, p. 19.

in their own country. When the Pan American Conference
met in Mexico in 1901-1902, the dictator forbade Indians
to be employed at any of the hotels housing the visitors,
lest these get the idea that Mexico was an Indian country.

The *Pax Porfiriana* was a Golden Age for foreigners,
whose investments were protected; Mexico became a
preserve for foreign capitalism. But the massive dictatorship was beginning to crumble. The 1907 depression in
the United States was felt in Mexico, and Díaz and his
coterie of retainers were old. In 1910 the dictator was 80,
two of his twenty state governors were over 80, and some
were past 70. Yet the regime and its beneficiaries seemed
to believe that the show would never end. On September
16, 1910, the one-hundredth anniversary of Mexico's independence and Díaz's 80th birthday were celebrated in
regal style. Thousands of guests and visitors poured into
the capital for the happy event. Díaz, the genial host, spent
$20 million of the nation's funds on fireworks, military
parades, banquets, music, speeches, and carloads of
champagne. The guests could see how cultured and con-
tented the Mexican people were; the city's poor and bare-
foot Indians were barred from the center of the capital.
When Díaz was again declared "elected" President on
September 27, 1910, the storm broke and the most important event of twentieth-century Mexico began—the
Revolution.

"Tierra y Libertad." With this hope of the people,
"land and liberty," the tumult began and for ten years
Mexico was in a confused uproar, with Francisco Madero,
Emiliano Zapata, Pancho Villa, Venustiano Carranza, and
other revolutionary leaders playing their various roles on
the crowded scene. One of the best volumes to convey
the feeling of this period is the collection of remarkable
photographs with captions, entitled *The Wind that Swept
Mexico*.[21]

The greatest achievement of the period was the drawing
up and the promulgation of the Constitution of 1917 by
a convention summoned by Carranza, who had emerged
by 1915 as the strongest of the revolutionary leaders. This
legal basis for the Revolution, which held and still holds

[21] Anita Brenner and George Leighton, *The Wind that Swept
Mexico. The History of the Mexican Revolution, 1910-
1942,* New York: Harper & Brothers, 1943.

much the same mystical authority and practical power as the U.S. Constitution, was a product of Mexican history, forged for Mexican purposes; it was an improvement and renewal, in large part, of the 1857 Constitution. It went beyond the 1857 document, however, in its effort to establish a planned agrarian and industrial system.

Article 3 made all public education secular and the primary grades compulsory, thus declaring the nation independent from the educational monopoly of the Church. Article 27 denied the ownership of land in fee simple; land belonged to the nation, including all subsoil minerals and petroleum, which could be exploited only by Mexican nationals or foreigners who agreed "to consider themselves as nationals" and not to invoke the protection of their governments. This vital article also aimed to restore to the Mexican people the lands alienated by previous laws, especially those of Díaz. Article 123 has been termed the Magna Carta of Mexican labor; it recognized labor's right to organize, bargain collectively, and strike. Labor was also promised the eight-hour day, the end of child labor, control of wages, equal pay for equal work, and responsibility of the employer in cases of occupational accidents and diseases.

The Constitution of 1917 in effect declared war on all the most powerful groups of the past: the clergy, the hacendados, and employers. It also gave stern warning to the United States, Great Britain, and other foreign states whose citizens had exploited Mexican land, oil fields, and mines. Its pronouncements have influenced the course of events in Chile, Colombia, and other Latin American republics faced with similar problems.

Under Carranza the Revolution got under way even though he exhibited little pride in the constitution he had theoretically fathered and did little to implement it; his generals devoted themselves to battening on the public purse. Carranza had that honest revolutionist Zapata shot, and carried on a continuous debate with President Woodrow Wilson, who had recognized his government in October, 1915, despite the loud cries of U.S. landowners, oil companies, and churchmen against "godless and socialistic Mexico." Opposition to Carranza mounted on all sides when the country saw that he intended to name his successor. He realized that his time was up, filled a twenty-car train with sacks of bullion and other loot, and thus equipped set out for Veracruz. Although one of his previous supporters arranged an attack on the train, he escaped into the mountains only to be trapped and murdered there by one of his own officers. With his death in May, 1920, the first phase of the Mexican Revolution was over.

The Era of Obregón and Calles. Comparative peace returned to Mexico when General Alvaro Obregón came to power in 1920. He was the first President to give a strong impetus to the social revolution by encouraging trade union organization, a modest program of land distribution, and education. José Vasconcelos, Minister of Education, undertook, with imagination and in a spirit of creative optimism, the gigantic task of teaching the Mexican masses. Vasconcelos, who respected both the European and Indian past, printed Spanish translations of Plato and Aristotle, and also established a thousand rural schools on a new pattern. The new rural school he called *La Casa del Pueblo* (The House of the People), and he designed it to serve the entire life of the village as a permanent educational mission offering a program of the three R's, music, painting, sports, theater, and practical instruction in sanitation and scientific agriculture.

Under Vasconcelos, too, the artists of Mexico were encouraged to paint murals on the walls of public buildings and thus to carry their interpretations of Mexico's epic struggle to the people. New World art must be popular art, declared José Clemente Orozco. (*See Reading No. 7.*) Diego Rivera and David Siqueiros were other great names in this movement; they organized an artists' union and stood on their scaffolds with conspicuous pistols to prove that they too belonged to the Revolution. Vasconcelos also launched Carlos Chávez on his distinguished musical career by commissioning a ballet. Although Vasconcelos later turned conservative, he preserved until his death in the summer of 1959 an individual and frank approach toward Mexico.

Obregón's political troubles were many. He was recognized by the United States only late in 1923; increasing difficulties with the Church led him to expel the apostolic delegate, Archbishop Filippi, and he could retain army support only by creating many new generals and overlooking their flagrant pilfering. "When General Francisco Serrano, his minister of war, lost 80,000 pesos in one sitting at the gaming tables, Obregón approved payment of the sum from the Treasury." [22] Even so, a revolt occurred when Obregón announced his support of Plutarco Elías Calles as his successor. But the uprising was suppressed and Obregón finished his presidential term in peace.

Calles was inaugurated December 1, 1924, amidst colorful ceremonies in which Indians, peasants, and industrial workers, fetched at public expense from the far corners of Mexico, mingled with several hundred U.S. labor leaders led by Samuel Gompers, the veteran President of the American Federation of Labor. The social revolution continued, not without bitter disputes concerning its direction and pace. The C.R.O.M. (*Confederación Regional Obrera Mexicana*) was given a practical monopoly over labor, road and irrigation programs were launched, the rural school program continued, and the National Bank of Mexico was established. The army was kept under control by strict discipline.

Although sorely tried by the threatened internal disintegration of the country due to conflicting ideas in the revolutionary family and by corruption in many quarters, Calles took a firm stand in his argument with the United States over oil and agrarian legislation. This controversy brought the two countries close to war. Dwight W. Morrow, U.S. Ambassador beginning in 1927, decisively improved relations and the oil and land disputes were eventually resolved.

One of Calles' greatest struggles was with the Church. Open warfare developed when it became clear that he meant to enforce strictly the anti-clerical provisions of the Constitution; he deported foreign priests, closed Church schools and convents, and accused the hierarchy of treason. In protest, the priests withdrew from their altars on July 31, 1926, and for the first time since 1519 no public Mass was celebrated in all Mexico. For almost three years the grim struggle went on. Through it all the faithful came to pray in the empty churches and some families with large houses smuggled in priests in lay garb to celebrate Mass behind drawn curtains—services in which the wives of leading revolutionaries, including Calles,

[22] Herring, *A History of Latin America,* p. 364.

participated. In 1929 the government reached a settlement with the Church, with some discreet assistance by Ambassador Morrow.

The tense election of 1928 brought a large number of opposition candidates into the field, but Obregón won, with Calles' support, despite great popular opposition. The newly elected president was killed by a young religious fanatic before he could take office, and Calles was in practical control for the next six years through men whom he named for the presidency and then dominated. This dreary period for Mexico and for the Revolution has been described by Frank Tannenbaum as "debased and clouded years" in which the revolutionary leaders failed. "They had risked their lives for the redemption of the people from poverty and serfdom. . . . Their difficulty lay in the fact that they had come to power suddenly and without preparation, either morally, psychologically, politically, or even administratively. They were taken from their villages as barefooted youngsters who had slept on the floor and could barely read, and after a few years spent on the battlefields found themselves tossed in high office and great responsibility. This new world was filled with a thousand temptations they had not dreamed of: gold, women, houses, carpets, diamonds, champagne. . . . It was a world of fable, and in their innocence and hunger—or greed, it does not matter—they succumbed to it. They succumbed to it because they had no moral fortitude. They had no philosophy and no faith, no system of values, no sense of the big world. The big world, especially the big city, was too much for them." [23]

In his struggle to bring political equilibrium to a country wracked by contending elements and ideas and deprived of a leader—Obregón—who had at least kept the intricate machine of Mexican political life ticking, Calles took a decisive step. He formed in 1929 an "official party"—*Partido Nacional Revolucionario*—in order to bind together the numerous regional and state political organizations and bosses so that a small group might prearrange elections and write legislation before it reached the halls of Congress. The president changes,

[23] Frank Tannenbaum, *Mexico: The Struggle for Peace and Bread,* New York: Alfred A. Knopf, 1950, pp. 69-70.

and thus the "no re-election" slogan is kept intact, but the party maintains control in a single-party state. Yet, as Howard Cline points out, "simultaneously Mexico preserves a full roster of civil liberties—free speech, free press, free assembly. Only the right to successful revolution is limited in fact." [24] No political machinery can run itself; the man who assured the party the dominance in Mexican life that it still enjoys was the most interesting and powerful figure the Revolution produced—General Lázaro Cárdenas.

Cárdenas Implements the Revolution, 1934-1940. The new president took office in December, 1934, for a six-year term by grace of Calles, but quickly ejected his protector and henchmen from the government. By June, 1935, Cárdenas controlled the nation more certainly than ever Díaz had done, and, unlike the dictator, enjoyed popular support even greater than that of Juárez. The people believed in this dedicated and modest President who gave his attention to the problems of Mexico and Mexicans beyond the glittering lights of the national and state capitals.

From this position of strength Cárdenas declared that the Revolution had not yet been effected, and began to put into effect a Six-Year Plan. He transferred some 45,000,000 acres of land to villages, twice as much land as had been distributed up to 1934; he found strong support for his program from a new labor union he sponsored, the CTM (*Confederación de Trabajadores Mexicanos*) led by Vicente Lombardo Toledano; and in June, 1937, he nationalized most of the railroads. He turned the nationalized roads over to a committee of railway unions to run, which compounded the confusion but, in the opinion of most Mexicans, was preferable to foreign control.

It was his expropriation of the properties of seventeen foreign oil companies on March 18, 1938, that won for Cárdenas the permanent title of defender of the sovereignty of the nation; the date became an annual occasion for celebration of Mexico's "Declaration of Economic Independence." The legal arguments involved were compli-

[24] Howard F. Cline, *The United States and Mexico,* Cambridge: Harvard University Press, 1953, p. 198.

cated and somewhat unclear, but the essential fact was
that Mexico believed the foreign companies had shown
disrespect for Mexico and her laws, and thus there could
be no retreat with honor. The presence of a friendly U.S.
ambassador, Josephus Daniels, the determination of President F. D. Roosevelt and Under Secretary of State Sumner
Welles to make the Good Neighbor Policy work, and the
already looming shadow of World War II all combined
to make a peaceful solution possible, Mexico agreed to
pay for the oil properties within ten years, and the U.S.
government recognized Mexico's right of expropriation
upon "adequate, effective, and prompt payment."

President Cárdenas completed his turbulent term of
office and settled down to life as the conscience of the
Revolution; his radical policies were hotly debated inside
as well as outside of Mexico, but few anywhere questioned
his integrity. He still towers above all the other revolutionary leaders.

The Revolution Slows Down. In 1940 Mexico
turned right, and has moved in this direction ever since.
Under Manuel Ávila Camacho (1940-1946), Mexico
joined the United States against the Axis and began to
develop her economy, particularly industry. The war years
saw inflation, a recrudescence of the rightist and religious
movement now called *Sinarquismo,* as well as a continuation of educational progress and the founding of a Social
Security Institute. Lombardo Toledano was ousted from
his labor post and anti-Communist leaders assumed
charge.

The Catholic Church regained much influence in this
period. The provisions of the Constitution of 1917
severely restricting Church, economic, educational, and
political activities have not been seriously invoked since
1940 when President Ávila Camacho declared publicly
"I am a believer." Today Catholic churches and seminaries
flourish; schools which used to function secretly are now
out in the open, though they have been named after
Mexican patriots instead of saints. Yet Mexico, like Latin
America generally, has a very low number of priests in
relation to communicants. Protestant groups are also
active throughout the Republic, and they claim 2 million
adherents. One of these groups, a U.S. organization, is

translating the Bible into various Indian languages with some 180 translators at work. Mixtec, Tzeltal, and Totonac versions have been published; Chol and Mazateco editions are on the way.

Under Miguel Alemán (1946-1952) the official party was re-baptized the *Partido de la Revolución Institucional,* as if to show that the Revolution had indeed been won and was now a sacred institution. Alemán vigorously pushed agricultural development, with technical aid from the Rockefeller Foundation, invigorated Pemex, the nationalized petroleum monopoly, and constructed an impressive University City on the edge of the capital. But his principal concern was the promotion of industry and, with the help of *Nacional Financiera,* a government finance corporation, by 1950 some 50,000 industrial concerns of many different types had been established. Alemán and his official family became famous for the upsurge of corruption which accompanied the material advance of Mexico; the *mordida* (bite) became an institution as sacred as the Revolution itself.

Adolfo Ruiz Cortines (1952-1958) continued the policies of his two predecessors. During his administration labor leader Fidel Velázquez built up the CTM to 1,500,-000 members, and organized the Labor Unity Bloc to strengthen government control over labor and combat communist infiltration. When Adolfo López Mateos was elected President in July, 1958, his success in averting all labor strikes as Secretary of Labor was expected to stand him in good stead. Yet in August a university student strike against city bus fare increases led to street riots in Mexico City where labor dissidents joined the students. Demetrio Vallejo, one-time Communist Party member, won control of the railroad workers later in the year in a nationwide strike, pulled them out of the Unity Bloc, and in February, 1959, called another strike and forced major wage concessions. Teachers, oil workers, telephone workers, and electrical workers are also involved in this struggle for the control of approximately 2 million trade unionists. Leftists are making some headway in their effort to break the government dominance of the labor unions, which they claim serve governmental ends rather than the workers. Vallejo clearly miscalculated his power, however,

in Easter Week, 1959, by calling a railroad strike which
stranded thousands of vacationers on holiday. Popular indignation enabled the government to crack down on the
left-wing labor leaders responsible. Two Soviet diplomats
were ordered expelled from Mexico on charges of involvement in the strike. The police moved into the railroad
union's headquarters in Mexico City with tear gas and
truncheons, arrested Vallejo and about 200 of his followers, and broke the strike. Both the Electrical Workers
Union and the Petroleum Workers Union, previously
united with Vallejo in a leftist bloc, disassociated themselves from Vallejo's actions and announced support for
the government's move against the railroad strike which
they said "had its roots abroad." Inflation and resentment
of large industrial profits are also elements in the situation;
a shift of power within the revolutionary family seems
to be involved, too.

Evidence of another possible shift is López Mateos'
attack on provincial dictators such as Gonzalo Natividad
Santos in San Luis Potosí, Leobardo Reynoso in Zacatecas,
and Margarito Ramírez in Quintana Roo. In the early
revolutionary days local strong men (caciques) staked out
a territory and ruled over it at gunpoint with the aid of
their henchmen called pistoleros, extorting taxes and
collecting bribes systematically. López Mateos announced
opposition to them during his campaign, but he must
move slowly, for the official party has been sustained by
these local bosses. Santos, for example, delivered his
province's vote for the party for twenty years and has
handpicked the governors, mayors, and congressmen
from San Luis Potosí. If labor and the state bosses no
longer are to be counted upon as solid supporters of the
party, its future may become uncertain.

The most important question in Mexico today, however,
is the extent to which the Revolution has succeeded and
failed.

Has the Revolution Succeeded? Most Mexicans,
and foreigners too, hold strong opinions on this subject.
The purpose of the Revolution was never closely defined;
inevitably sharply contrasting opinions are held. The
deep-seated and widespread corruption in government
distresses many Mexicans; the mordant writer Daniel
Cosío Villegas considers the moral anarchy he sees every-

where a great threat to the development of the nation. Not only has the Revolution failed to lead Mexico toward effective democracy, declares J. L. Mecham, but it has failed even to raise the level of political morality.[25] One American professor who held high hopes for the success of the Revolution in its early agrarian days, is now clearly disappointed, believing that "a mood of cynicism has taken hold of the country, especially in the cities." [26]

Those who believe that the democratic level of a country is indicated by the quality of the men willing to serve it point to Agustín Yáñez, recently governor of Jalisco for six years, as an example of a disinterested and competent public servant. Called Mexico's greatest living novelist, he gave himself wholeheartedly to meet the many pressing problems of his powerful and turbulent state, listened to the people, persuaded politicos and others not to carry pistols, and when asked to comment on his role as Governor said: "Government calls for the essential quality of the novelist: imagination."

Others just as aware of certain unsavory and unsatisfactory aspects of Mexican life since Díaz was driven out in 1910 consider that, on balance, the Revolution may be fully justified "before the conscience of the man of today and tomorrow." For "there are two completely positive factors to be noted, particularly since 1935; respect for human life and freedom of thought. At this moment, we can say with satisfaction, there are no political prisoners in any part of the national territory; everyone can express his ideas, whatever they may be, without danger; one can attack the government, one can even attack the President anywhere; one can write against the authorities; nothing will happen to the writer, the orator, the agitator." [27]

[25] J. Lloyd Mecham, "An Appraisal of the Mexican Revolution," A. Curtis Wilgus, ed., *The Caribbean at Mid-Century,* Gainesville: University of Florida Press, 1951, pp. 170-201.

[26] Tannenbaum, *Mexico: The Struggle for Peace and Bread,* p. 244.

[27] Jesús Silva Herzog, *Un ensayo sobre la revolucion mejicana,* in Benjamin Keen, ed., *Readings in Latin-American Civilization,* Boston: Houghton Mifflin Co., 1955, pp. 364-370, *passim.*

Although discussion of the Revolution leads to no generally accepted conclusion, nearly everyone agrees that it has ended. It is now the object of historical investigation; bibliographies are being compiled, documents published, generals' memoirs collected, and a new day is dawning for those who study the history of modern Mexico. But though "the Revolution" is dead, another great transformation is under way and its name is industrialization.

Mexico Forges Ahead.   The story of Mexican economic growth since 1940 is one of advance on many fronts. Agricultural production has nearly tripled, although only one-third more land has been put under cultivation. Cotton production has shot up sixfold, to become both the country's number one crop in value and its leading export; Mexico is now the world's second largest exporter of cotton. The second crop is coffee; Mexico is the third largest coffee producer in Latin America.

Petroleum supplies 85 per cent of the energy consumed in the country, and most of Mexico's more than 300,000-barrel daily production is used nationally. Mining has been slow, but recent tax exemptions are expected to encourage exploitation of lower grade minerals and investment in metal-producing plants.

The greatest change has come in industry, in which manufacturing, no longer limited to textiles and food processing as before the war, now includes some producer goods as well as consumer goods ranging from instant coffee and plastic gadgets to refrigerators. Between 1950 and 1956 manufacturing rose 62 per cent in volume; increase in real national output has averaged 7 per cent a year. One of the disadvantages of industrialization has already been experienced in Mexico City. A March, 1959, report by Unesco scientists shows that 200 tons of smoke are released there every day; the haze that hangs over the city is not as aggressive as the smog of Los Angeles or the fog of London, but it grows thicker every year.

Matamoros and Culiacán doubled in population between 1940 and 1950; the four largest cities, Mexico City, Guadalajara, Monterrey, and Puebla, grew more than 5 per cent a year since 1940. Of special significance, states Antonio Carrillo Flores who presents a favorable view of Mexican development, "has been the rise of a progressive middle class, whose attitudes and habits of work and saving are self-important to an expanding market economy." [28]

Yet certain disquieting facts emerge. A Mexican economist declares that, although the national production has definitely risen 50 per cent since 1945, half the population has a standard of living no higher than it was fifty years ago.[29] Another economist, Manuel Germán Parra, points out that the distribution of income was more unequal in 1955 than in 1940; 100,000 industrialists and businessmen in 1955 received 36,000 millions of pesos, while 10 million workers had 28,000 millions of the national income. Thus the ordinary worker participates very little in the expanded Mexican economy.

The drive to industrialize has led to the relative neglect of agriculture, some believe, though important improvements have been effected. Irrigation, better seeds, fertilizers, pest control, and mechanization have resulted in improved agricultural production. Yet less than 10 per cent of Mexico's largely mountainous and desert terrain is arable, and of this land 80 per cent is so arid that only about half of the cultivable soil is actually farmed. Many small plots of land are worked by primitive methods not likely to be abandoned without a tremendous educational campaign and investment in seeds, fertilizers, and machinery. The differences are striking between the "new agriculture" in the north and northwest where large-scale farming with modern equipment is carried on, and the *"minifundia"* of the other parts of Mexico where almost a million families cultivate holdings of less than 5 hectares, according to the 1950 census.

The early extravagant hopes that merely dividing up the large estates would solve the problem have now disappeared. Land distribution slowed down after 1939, although it continued at a substantial rate for some years. In the face of loud cries of "betraying the Revolution," the government adopted the policy of price pegging, support for independent farmers, and the feverish construction of dams and irrigation systems to assure cheap water.

[28] "Mexico Forges Ahead," *Foreign Affairs,* XXXVI (New York, 1958), pp. 491-502.

[29] Quoted by Oscar Lewis in a valuable, succinct summary, "México desde 1940," *Investigación Económica* XVII (Mexico City, 1958), No. 70, p. 230.

The campaign worked and by 1950 Mexico was producing enough maize, beans, rice, and sugar to feed her own people. Mexico imported in 1944 more than 300,000 tons of wheat annually; in 1955 it was officially announced that imports of wheat would be unnecessary because of the great increase in national production. The Rockefeller Foundation was a powerful influence in making this increase possible.

The further distribution of land to landless peasants will not necessarily increase production greatly. The most publicized distribution of land to peasants both on an organized communal basis (*ejidos*) and as private operators took place in the fertile Laguna district in north central Mexico. A recent investigation indicates that cotton and wheat production have definitely increased there since expropriation but "the increase, ironically enough has come mostly from the private properties. Their owners have been forced to intensify cultivation, using wells and machinery to a higher degree than before." [30] The United Nations announced for 1959-1960 an investigation of the actual results of land reform in underdeveloped countries, including Mexico, which will be based not on official sources alone but also upon information provided by technical experts and academic research centers. The Bank of Mexico considers that conclusions based upon nonofficial reports may be more accurate than the often rosy picture drawn by government agencies. [31]

The luxury residences in the modern suburbs of Mexico's rapidly growing cities illustrate one dramatic aspect of her economy, the conspicuous consumption practiced by businessmen in trade, industry, finance, and government who have reaped a paper if not a golden harvest and choose to spend some of their inflation-born gains rather than to invest them in the further development of industry. Throughout Mexico, however, live many people whose tools and techniques have remained largely the same since the days of Montezuma. According to one anthropologist, these folk "have taken many new traits of modern life. They now have Coca-Cola, aspirin, radios, sewing machines, phonographs, poolrooms, flashlights, clocks, steel plows, and some labor-saving devices. They

[30] Senior, *Land Reform and Democracy,* p. 189.
[31] "Land Reform," *Reseña Económica y Tecnológica,* vol. V (Banco de México, March, 1959), No. 57, p. 209.

also have a greater desire to attend school, to eat better, to dress better, and to spend more. But in many ways their world view is still much closer to sixteenth-century Spain and to pre-Hispanic Mexico than to the modern scientific world. They are still guided by superstition and primitive beliefs; sorcery, magic, evil winds, and spirits still dominate their thinking. It is clear that, for the most part, they have taken on only the more superficial aspects and values of modern life. . . ." [32]

Mexico is forging ahead, of this there can be no doubt, and the need for a balance between agriculture and industry is recognized by her leaders. The Mexican economy has developed more rapidly and more uniformly than the economy of any other Latin American country; many Mexicans are convinced that they have found the formula for a balanced growth which will soon take Mexico out of the category of "underdeveloped country." But the enthusiastic reports of progress must be assessed in the light of the acute analysis of the facts worked out by her growing body of trained economists.

President Ruiz Cortines, in his annual report for 1956, has expressed well the need to avoid excessive optimism when he stated: "We are advancing, indeed; but our population is also increasing, sometimes more rapidly than our national product. We are progressing, it is true; but the progress which we have made as a nation permits us to see more clearly the condition of those who are not participating in our increased prosperity, and of those who are not benefitting as much as we could desire. It is painful for me to think of the enormous masses who still suffer in ignorance, enduring poverty and unhealthful conditions. As long as these masses do not advance at the same rate as the rest of the nation we will have to say to those who are satisfied with our progress that we have as yet accomplished little, since we have not fulfilled our main objective." [33]

[32] Oscar Lewis, *Life in a Mexican Village: Tepozotlán Restudied*, Urbana: University of Illinois Press, 1951, pp. 447-448.

[33] *Informe que rinde al H. Congreso de la Unión el C. Presidente de la República Adolfo Ruiz Cortines. Correspondiente a su gestión del 1° de septiembre de 1955 al 31 de agosto de 1956*, Mexico City: Secretaría de Gobernación, 1956, p. 93.

A 1958 report by the Director General of Statistics documents this statement in cold, arithmetical terms: "3,700,000 families or approximately 18,500,000 Mexicans live precariously, for their income is always less than their expenditure; thus they have no opportunity to save and live in permanent debt." [34]

Mexico and the United States. Most of Mexico's international trade is with the United States, and the half million tourists who have gone south each year since World War II for recreation and stimulation provide Mexico with an important source of foreign exchange which now brings in half as much as Mexico derives from all her exports. U.S. private investment today comes to some $700 millions, about the same dollar investment as at the beginning of the Revolution, but now U.S. investments represent a much larger percentage of total foreign investments than in the earlier period. The nature of the investment has also changed radically; mining, railroads, and oil have yielded first place to manufacturing. Many of the large business enterprises are in U.S. hands, a predominance which has been characterized by a Mexican group as "a serious menace to the integrity of the nation and to the freedom of the country to project its own economic development." [35]

Opposition to U.S. investment unites many diverse elements—nationalists, small manufacturers, intellectuals, and industrialists—but such a financial expert as Alfredo Navarrete, Jr., Director of Economic Investigations for the powerful government investment agency Nacional Financiera, has recently argued that Mexico must foster greater investment by Mexicans but must also attract foreign funds such as are available in the great insurance companies of the world. He feels that Mexico's economy needs more capital, and that the country is sufficiently strong to use foreign capital with profit and without danger.[36]

[34] "Ingresos y egresos de la población de México," *Reseña Económica y Tecnológica,* vol. V (Banco de México, February, 1959), No. 56, p. 175.

[35] Lewis, *México desde 1940,* p. 207.

[36] Alfredo Navarrete, Jr., "Una política de inversiones extranjeras," *Comercio Exterior,* VII (Mexico City: August, 1958), No. 8, pp. 421-424.

This well-reasoned, confident proposal, based on Mexico's needs and Mexico's capabilities, is a far cry from the 1941 pronouncements of such economists as Eduardo Villaseñor who predicted that the United States must export private capital to Latin America. "You may even have to give your capital away," he said, "lest you become a modern Midas and witness the decline and fall of the United States in the midst of a golden age of plenty—with all your gold interred somewhere in the Union.

"I say, then: get rid of your Treasure—lend it, give it, throw it away—if you do not want to perish in the midst of plenty." [37] Even today some Mexican economists apparently hold that underdeveloped countries such as Mexico would be doing the United States a favor by taking aid "to maintain employment in the U.S." [38] And always some Mexican voices are heard which reflect a desire to unify Latin America against the United States, or to assume a semi-neutralist position in the contest between Russia and the United States. (*See Readings Nos. 4,8.*)

"Mexico has one international problem; it is a permanent one, serious and sometimes grave," asserts one of Mexico's outstanding figures, and this problem arises because Mexico borders on the United States, "the most powerful nation of the earth in modern times; and this country is imperialistic, an economic phenomenon which results from its formidable financial and industrial development." [39]

Relations between the two countries have markedly improved, however, since 1940. Mexicans now have greater confidence in their own strength, and greater contact has brought greater understanding in many areas.

[37] Eduardo Villaseñor ' "Inter-American Trade and Financial Problems," in Walter H. C. Laves, ed., *Inter-American Solidarity,* Chicago: University of Chicago Press, 1941, pp. 93-94.

[38] Pobrecito, "Development, Scientific Pretension, and the Need for a Policy of the Informed Neighbor," *Inter-American Economic Affairs,* X (Washington, D.C., 1956), No. 3, pp. 43-59.

[39] Jesús Silva Herzog, "Meditaciones sobre México," *Cuadernos Americanos,* XXXV (Mexico City: September-October, 1947), p. 34.

Anti-Yankee sentiment in the rural areas and among the urban poor apparently scarcely exists, while the rising middle class emulates U.S. mores and values. A recent study conducted by psychologists concerning the attitude of Mexican school children toward the United States revealed the surprising result that 57 per cent of the boys and 67 per cent of the girls responded affirmatively when asked simply whether they would like to be North Americans.[40] Friction over treatment of the agricultural workers that stream yearly across the border to perform "stoop-labor" in the fields of California, Texas, and other states has notably diminished. According to L. B. Simpson, this remarkable migration may prove to be—despite the abuses practiced on some of the workers while in the United States—"the most effective program in international education that could be devised." [41] The Mexicans are excellent workmen, naturally courteous, and help to dispel the ignorance and prejudice existing in some U.S. circles. The Mexicans return with more than savings, automobiles, clothing, refrigerators; they also have new techniques and new ideas, and a generally friendly attitude to the United States. At any rate, the problem is no longer a danger to Mexican-U.S. relations.

Intellectuals oriented toward Europe and small industrialists who fear competition from the great U.S. firms maintain the traditional suspicion or at least reserve toward the United States. And many Mexicans view with apprehension what they call the "cocacolonization" of Mexican culture, by which they mean a wide variety of cultural influences from the north that range from "Santa Claus to psychoanalysis." Mexico, then, feels the economic and social influence of the United States, but she has become more capable of resisting it or at least using it in her own way. Her own deep and richly variegated culture exists more strongly than ever before. In fact,

---

[40] Guillermo Dávila, *et al.,* "Image of Americans in the Mexican Child," *Psychological Approaches to Inter-group and Inter-national Understanding* (Austin: Hogg Foundation for Mental Hygiene, The University of Texas, 1956), p. 35.

[41] Lesley B. Simpson, *Many Mexicos,* 3rd ed., Berkeley: University of California Press, 1952, pp. 312-313.

Mexico has never had as interesting and lively a development in art, letters, philosophy, and science as today.

Ramón Beteta has proposed that Mexico become the interpreter of Latin America to the United States. Señor Beteta has served in virtually every Mexican Cabinet since the administration of President Cárdenas, in which he was one of the brain trusters behind the oil expropriation. He suggests that Mexico, as a nation which won its own revolution, enjoys the confidence and respect of the rest of Latin America, and is a neighbor and friend of the United States, can help Washington understand the crisis through which Latin America is passing.

Certainly President Eisenhower's visit to President López Mateos in February, 1959, was a public affirmation of continuing good relations between the countries. And Mexicans had the satisfaction of not only celebrating in April, 1959, the 21st birthday of the oil expropriation, but also of announcing shortly afterward that the national oil industry, Pemex, had received a private loan of $40 million from four U.S. banks and subsequently another loan of $20 million from the European Common Market fund.

Mexican Culture Today.   Nineteenth-century Mexicans tended to depreciate their own achievements, to believe that these were innately inferior to those of Europe. Beginning with the Revolution, Mexicans began to appreciate their own culture. Wars disillusioned many with respect to Europe and a new national sense of their own culture, distinct from that of Europe, was born. "And in turning its back on Europe, Mexico has availed itself of the ideas of nationalism . . . a European concept." [42] This movement quickly came to be the dominant voice in art, literature, music, philosophy. Book stores, art galleries, and historical museums sprang up, and cultural missions were despatched to the provinces to shed light there. "Mexican character" was probed; the one most powerful and persistent theme in this upsurge of national spirit was the inquiry into what it means to be a Mexican in the contemporary world. [43] Mexican culture is heter-

[42] Samuel Ramos, *Perfil de la cultura mexicana,* 2nd ed., Mexico City: Editorial Pedro Robredo, 1938, pp. 136-137.

[43] John L. Phelan, "México y lo Mexicano," *Hispanic American Historical Review,* XXXVI (1956), pp. 309-318.

ogeneous and defies neat categorization, but one notable characteristic has been an intense concern with itself, at times almost amounting to narcissism. (*See Reading No. 34.*)

A trend away from "Mexicanism" toward a more universalistic approach is now in progress. The Spanish intellectuals, who brought their knowledge and skills to Mexico after Franco triumphed in Spain, helped to bring the thought of the world to Mexico. That extraordinary publishing house, the *Fondo de Cultura Económica,* has laid down a broad foundation for the cultural development of Mexico by providing excellent translations of substantial foreign books in many fields and by offering Mexican writers an opportunity to be heard. The legitimate theater in Mexico City has also been a cosmopolitan influence in recent years. In 1950 there were only three theaters, but in 1958 thirty were in full swing. Some are small and intimate; the *Teatro de los Insurgentes* seats 1,200 and is one of the most perfectly equipped in Latin America, and the government-built Cultural Unity Center in Chapultepec Park holds 18,000. In recent years some of the finest plays of other countries have been produced. The percentage of foreign importations has been so high that the intense nationalists have raised their ancient banner with a new motto: "Mexican theaters for Mexican authors." [44]

Since about 1956 a lively polemic has been under way with Communists and nationalists shouting the long-popular slogan "Mexico for the Mexicans!" At times it appeared that all writing and art which did not directly deal with the exploitation of the Mexican Indian, peasant, or wet-back was to be labelled anti-Mexican and a subservience to base American imperialist aggression. In the newly established *Revista de Literatura Mexicana* and elsewhere, Emanuel Carballo, Octavio Paz, Jorge Portilla, and others have decried chauvinistic nationalism in any field and defended brilliantly the right of Mexicans to complete freedom of artistic expression and to acceptance of influences from abroad. They believe that the Mexican creative spirit should flower in any field it wishes and its products should be made known to the world.

[44] Allan Lewis, "The Theater in Mexico," *The Texas Quarterly,* vol. II (University of Texas, 1959), No. 1, p. 145.

Art exhibits are sent to New York, Paris, and Stockholm; a young but able and dedicated ballet group performed in Russia, and the symphony orchestra had a highly successful European tour in 1958. Members of the so-called "third generation" of music composers, such as Raúl Cosío, do not feel that they must draw exclusively upon Mexico's rich treasury of folk music for their themes.[45] Orozco early in his career mocked at those who allowed politics to dominate their art; the young painter José Luis Cuevas expresses today his feeling thus: "What I want in my country's art are broad highways leading out to the rest of the world, rather than narrow trails connecting one adobe village with another." (*See Reading No. 35.*)

Mexicans today not only preach universalism; Mexico has also produced such a figure as the writer Alfonso Reyes, judged by many inside and outside Mexico to be the most complete, the most universal Mexican, who died in December, 1959, after a full and exciting life. Reyes taught his countrymen to prize their own arts while remaining fully aware of other cultures. Mexico remains faithful to her Indian past—there has never yet been erected a public monument to Cortez in the republic while Cuauhtémoc has an imposing one in the capital—but her face is now turned toward the world. The poet Octavio Paz, one of the wisest interpreters of contemporary Mexico, has written: "The Mexican Revolution forced us to come out of ourselves and to face up to history, assigned to us the task of inventing our own future and our own institutions. The Mexican Revolution has died without having resolved our contradictions. After the Second World War we are realizing that this self-creation which our reality demands of us is identical with that which a similar reality demands of others. We live, like the rest of the planet, in a decisive and mortal era, orphans

[45] Horacio Flores Sánchez, "Los compositores rebeldes se presentan con su música," in "México en la cultura, No. 506," the Sunday cultural supplement in *Novedades* (Mexico City, November 24, 1958). This newspaper offers its readers each week well-written articles on various aspects of Mexican culture. Issue No. 500, October 12, 1958, gives a panoramic view of Mexican culture today.

of the past and with an uncharted future. Universal History is now a common task, and our labyrinth, the labyrinth of all mankind." [46]

Another noteworthy characteristic of Mexico today is the frank and steadfast gaze its writers and researchers direct to the realities of Mexican life and the critical powers they have developed to judge them. In 1937 Eyler N. Simpson remarked that the Mexican investigator who actually went out into the field to look for facts about his own country was so rare as to be a curiosity. "I could name on the fingers of one hand the research monographs dealing with modern social problems published by Mexican students in the last decade." [47] Now Lucio Mendieta y Núñez directs an active Institute of Social Investigations at the University, from which solid studies come regularly; professional reviews such as *El Trimestre Económico, Investigación Económica,* and *Revista Mexicana de Sociología* attract competent writers, while *Problemas Agrícolas e Industriales de México* provides a forum for active debate on Mexican needs. The latter publication frequently translates serious studies on Mexico, often by U.S. professors, and then invites leading Mexican scholars to comment. The result is a lively and valuable contribution to the clarification of ideas on important topics. Monographs such as José Iturriaga's *La estructura social y cultural de México* testify to the penetration and sophistication now available in Mexico for the study of the nation's society.

The development of a universal view of the world rooted in Mexican experience, and the determination to look squarely at the social facts of Mexican life may prove to be the greatest revolution of them all—a revolution testifying powerfully to the vigor and independence of the people of Mexico today.

Conclusion: From Marble Palace to University City. Just as one may climb Chapultepec Hill to gain perspective on the great city of Mexico, so one may stand amidst the dramatic new buildings of the oldest university of the Western Hemisphere and find another meaningful perspective on the present and future of the Republic.

[46] Octavio Paz, *El laberinto de la soledad,* Mexico City: Ediciones Cuadernos Americanos, 1950, pp. 168-169.
[47] Eyler N. Simpson, *The Ejido—Mexico's Way Out,* Chapel Hill: University of North Carolina Press, 1937, p. 579.

When Porfirio Díaz wished to impress the world with the heights of culture Mexico had attained under his rule, he began in 1900 a marble Palace of Fine Arts in the center of the capital—grandiose, expensive, with a colored glass stage curtain made by Tiffany of New York and complicated stage machinery from Germany. The guide book describes part of the ornate interior in these terms: "The dressing rooms of the stage artists are palatial boudoirs. There is a fine café and bar, a vast cellar filled with thousands of bottles of choice wines and liqueurs, a smoking room, and reception rooms, and *salons* that would grace a castle in Spain." [48] Today the Palace remains a strange monument to the period in which it was built, when its grandeur bore little relation to the lives and needs of most Mexicans. One may see a symbol in the fact that the marble edifice was so poorly suited to the subsoil conditions of Mexico City that it began to sink into the spongy ground before it was half-completed. The mass of the people were landless, lived miserably, and in any case they were not allowed to pass through the imposing main entrance on the Avenida Juárez. The only Indian seen by the top-hatted gentlemen and bejewelled ladies as they entered to attend some gala function was a melancholy, squatting basalt figure discovered in an eighteenth-century excavation and known as the *Indio Triste* (Sad Indian).

When Mexicans half a century later wished to erect a gigantic symbol of their position today, they constructed a University City on the hard black lava flow of great antiquity called the Pedregal. Modern, enormous in size (its stadium alone holds approximately 100,000 persons to surpass any university stadium in the United States) exultant in spirit, the Ciudad Universitaria dramatizes "Mexico's modernity, her technology, her resources and her power." [49]

The building of the university was a colossal undertaking, accomplished in a remarkably short time. Many of the architects and engineers in Mexico were mobilized for

[48] *Terry's Guide to Mexico,* Boston: Houghton Mifflin Co., 1935, pp. 327-328.

[49] Harwell Hamilton Harris, "Regionalism and Nationalism in Architecture," *The Texas Quarterly,* No. 1 (University of Texas Press, 1958), p. 123.

the task; some construction elsewhere had to be halted to make men and materials available for this great effort to stimulate the national pride and develop Mexico's technical and industrial resources so that future constructions might be erected by modern means—not by men in bare feet working with bare hands.

The University City does not in fact provide a particularly convenient campus for its 30,000 students and professors; communication on foot between the widely scattered buildings is laborious. Although the medical school might well be near the hospitals, this faculty was moved to the University City 10 miles south of the capital to swell the size of the total effect.

Harwell Hamilton Harris, an American architect, applauds the University City as a splendid example "of the dynamic function of architecture—of an architecture's power to embody the spirit of a nation in a symbol that her citizens recognize and that arouses them to further expressions of it," but he also wonders if some of the new architectural forms transplanted from Europe and adapted here—the thin vaults, the cantilevers, the stilts used to support some buildings—may not represent a possible "new colonialism." He concludes, with a warning which he believes to apply equally to New England and to Mexico: "An architecture that is only a symbol, and a borrowed symbol at that, is a china egg. It will not hatch—unless it stimulates the hen to lay a real egg it had better not be used. It will be a deterrent to the development of a living architecture." [50]

Mexicans raise questions and level criticisms, too, for neither persons nor institutions escape the rapier wit and merciless pens of Mexico's many writers and cartoonists. They point out that these splendid buildings were erected at the expense of the poorer and smaller provincial universities. And they note that within the stunningly decorated library's walls too few books have been provided for the students. But they are proud of the great undertaking and rejoice that university teaching is becoming, for the first time, a full-time profession. They see the flamboyance and variety of architectural styles brought together here and certain as yet unsolved problems as truly symbolic of the transitional state of Mexican culture.

Although Mexicans are the first to assert that much remains to be done in Mexico, much indeed has been achieved. The army has become the instrument of civilian thinking and direction; there has been no successful revolt in twenty-five years. Mexican governments have enforced discipline; in fact, some observers believe that the optimistic views earlier expressed on the state of civil liberties in Mexico should be revised. They feel that the former subtle control of press, speech, and assembly is today less subtle; the press is not wholly trusted, the president may not be attacked, and the single party keeps dissidents in line. The Revolution, which started out with the cry of *"Tierra y Libertad,"* they hold, has not only ended, but reversed itself. Large landholdings have come back, especially in the irrigated areas, though they are farmed much more scientifically than under the dictatorship of Porfirio Díaz. The socialist state which emerged from the Revolution has laid the foundation for full-scale modern capitalism.

The truth of these and other controversial opinions now held on Mexico will only be determined after the passage of more time. Meanwhile it is clear that the people for whom the Revolution was fought have not been forgotten, although their condition still requires great improvement. Most important of all, the Mexican nation has experienced a profound social revolution and has passed beyond it to achieve a special and Mexican kind of stability which gives it a unique position in Latin America.

6

CONCLUSION

A Marshall Plan for Latin America Is Not Enough.
Representatives of the 21 hemisphere governments wit-
nessed in Buenos Aires on April 13, 1959, the signing of
the charter of the billion Inter-American Bank for Development, for which the United States has provided $450
million. Thus began Operation Panamerica, a sort of
Marshall Plan, which Latin Americans have insistently
proposed for ten years.

If properly conducted, the new Bank should be help-
ful in many ways; if Latin American governments utilize
wisely the funds available to them from the Bank and
elsewhere, a break-through may be possible in some of the
economic difficulties that now beset them. But money
alone will not satisfy the younger generations in Latin
America who are now eager to see social and democratic
revolutions take place in their countries. These younger
groups have felt that the United States was blind or
indifferent to Latin American democratic yearnings; some
of them are also beginning to realize that they have a
responsibility to assume in their own countries.

It is well that favorable sentiment for economic aid to
Latin America has developed in the Washington administration and Congress. It is well that Congress has
authorized an investigation of U.S. policy in the area to
discover how our performance in this field can be improved. Equally significant are the kinds of public concern
being manifested in the United States as this book is being
written. The discussions and programs arranged by universities and other institutions will be effective, however,
only in so far as they take into account the special quality
of the ferment in Latin America. Revolution and revolt
are nothing new there; throughout 300 years of colonial
rule and the nineteenth century, disturbances occurred
frequently, although they are not all recorded in the

textbooks. Columbus was the first dictator, and Trujillo will not be the last, in the area included in this volume.

What is new today is the realignment of the traditional forces in Latin America. The army is no longer a merely military force; in some countries and to some degree, it is an enlightened instrument, desirous of national welfare, and aware of the complex, difficult social and economic issues that must be resolved. The Roman Catholic Church, too, no longer blindly supports dictators, nor is unmindful of the desperate need to improve the living conditions of the people. (*See Reading No. 6.*) Everywhere universities are being improved, so that their graduates may eventually bear the brunt of directing change, in a way their fathers, certainly their grandfathers, never dreamt of doing. Everywhere the middle classes are growing in numbers and importance; sometimes called "middle masses" or "middle sectors," they will undoubtedly wield greater political power in the future.

Latin Americans are no longer dominated by the former widespread awe of European culture; they are learning English, but this does not necessarily imply any fondness for the United States. They are a tough generation and will not be easy to deal with; no mere profit-making philosophy will move them, and rosy propaganda will be wasted on them. Some of them have yet to discover the intellectual resilience of U.S. culture, and the forces that defy standardization and complacency; they have not always been aware of the deep-flowing springs of our national life, evidenced by the 1954 decision of the Supreme Court on school integration, and by the battle-cries of our educational leaders determined to improve quality at a time when every facility is crowded from one-room schoolhouses to large state universities.

Explosion or Evolution? The searching discussion and debate now in progress in the hemisphere will undoubtedly become more widespread in the months ahead, and more frank. As Arturo Morales Carrión, Under Secretary of State of the Commonwealth of Puerto Rico, has said: "We are in for a big and tense debate in this Hemisphere on the true nature of inter-American relationships. While the dictators were in power, the press was muzzled. Any debate was highly artificial. Only those issues were argued which the dictator allowed to be debatable. But now the press has gained its freedom from Argentina to Cuba, and a searching analysis has begun. This is a battle of facts and ideas and it cannot be avoided. We who favor an effective, vigorous solidarity in the Americas, must brace ourselves for a period of critical questioning, covering every phase from politics to education, from cultural mores to economic development and the values of U.S. techniques." [51]

Latin Americans, too, must be ready for a more informed scrutiny of their actions than ever before; no emotional appeal to a mystic continental unity, no strident denunciation of U.S. support for dictators at a time when they also tolerate them, no refusal to take hard but necessary decisions in their own sphere of action, are likely to make much impression in the United States.

This discussion will be valueless if it deals in generalities without recognizing the complexity of the situation in the individual countries. This volume and its companion Anvil study on South America aim to provide some of the background that can help the facing of facts to be an invigorating wind rather than a destructive hurricane. Both volumes assume that thoughtful men and women, devoted to the establishment of truly democratic values in their own countries, whether in North or South America, must bring intelligence, determination, and good will to bear upon the national problems they all must admit exist. Only in this spirit can Americans of both hemispheres choose between the alternatives of our time: evolution or explosion.

[51] Remarks made by Dr. Morales at the Third National Conference on Exchange of Persons in Washington, D.C., January 30, 1959.

Part 2

SELECTED READINGS

~ Reading No. 1 ~

VISIBLE AND INVISIBLE AMERICA[1]

Germán Arciniegas has served in Colombia's diplomatic corps and has been Minister of Education for a brief period. As essayist, historian, and critic, he has written steadily and copiously. He has been a Professor in Columbia University, and is now the Ambassador in Italy of Colombia's bipartisan government. Always he has been preoccupied with freedom in the Americas.

✓ ✓ ✓

There are two Americas: the visible and the invisible. The visible America, the America of presidents and embassies, expresses itself through official organs, through a controlled press. This America takes its seat at the conference table of the Pan American Union and has many votes in the United Nations. And there is the mute, repressed America, which is a vast reservoir of revolution. Both Americas are misleading in appearance.

Under its dictatorial regimes, visible America makes fervent protestations of its democratic faith, signs charters of liberties, manufacturing one line of goods for foreign and another for domestic consumption. This double personality has achieved a dexterity that is almost unbelievable. Even though everywhere and in all periods of history there has been something of this same split between what is said and what is done, the contrast has rarely been so brutal as that afforded by the Latin American dictatorships. . . .

This arbitrary use of words has given rise to the

[1] Germán Arciniegas, *The State of Latin America,* New York; Alfred A. Knopf, 1952, pp. 386-392, *passim.*

greatest confusion. The despots use the word "democracy" to set up governments such as those described in the pages of this book. The common man asks himself if this can be democracy. The same thing holds true of the other words in the political lexicon: army, religion, freedom, Christianity, faith, republic, justice, judge, president, elections, congress, priest, university, peace, public opinion. By turning words inside out, dictators destroy the natural medium of communication between people. . . . There are peace and order because no one can talk or criticize or object or join his fellows in assembly. . . .

Theoretically it would seem that Latin America is a fertile field for Communism. Yet it is amazing how few addicts this party has made. . . . France has many more Communists than all Latin America despite the fact that the people of Latin America, badly fed, badly dressed, badly housed and badly treated, are in much closer contact than any other with the capitalism of their next-door neighbor. Why does Communism fail to take hold there? Because in Latin America the thirst for freedom is as great as the thirst for justice. Because there is a sense of national pride. The Mexican wants to be master of his own house, not the lackey of Moscow. . . .

Like visible America, invisible America lies. The humble folk know that they cannot say what they think, and the upper classes have learned this too. . . . In invisible America, where a vast mass of the population lives with the cold breath of terror on its neck, the least word may bring reprisals. The part of prudence is to keep quiet, to wear a mask. Where machine guns have the floor a deep silence reigns. Life goes on under the cover of conventional phrases, lip-service, extorted votes. . . . Nobody knows exactly what these 150,000,000 silent men and women think, feel, dream, or await in the depths of their being. . . .

Native capital flees from Latin America. Only in Montevideo and Mexico City have large fortunes found refuge. If the amount of Latin American funds on deposit today in the banks of New York and Switzerland were accurately known, one would conclude that Latin America possesses all the capital it needs. Even capital is invisible in America. . . .

With two Americas, visible and invisible, each having
a double personality, it is a region of complexities shot
through with reserves, suspicion, resentment, wariness and
fears. There is one word that arouses an immeasurable
reaction on the part of those who have emerged from a
colonial world . . . "intervention." . . . And throughout the hemisphere, in the background, stand the people.
The day they can make themselves heard there may be a
consuming fire or a flood of light.

— Reading No. 2 —

LATIN AMERICAN DEMOCRACY[2]

*Gonzalo J. Facio, one-time Costa Rican Ambassador
to the United States, was president of the Legislative
Assembly of his country from 1953 to 1955 and has also
headed the Costa Rican delegation to the U.N.*

✓   ✓   ✓

Some Latin Americans do not adequately understand
the United States as a new civilization. The people of the
earth are not used to swift changes. The rapid ascent of
the United States has left behind many minds, who are still
thinking in nineteenth-century European terms. These
persons are not ready to accept wholeheartedly North
American leadership in a program of hemispheric development. Others . . . expect too much of the United States
as a leader of the democratic cause. They would like to
see Latin America cleared of dictators and political ad-
venturers by a simplified formula through North American
pressure. Thus the United States government is torn be-

[2] Gonzalo J. Facio, "Latin American Democracy," *Colorado
Quarterly* (Autumn, 1957), pp. 120-123, *passim*. Reprinted by permission.

tween the call of democratic leadership and the doctrine of nonintervention. . . .

There is an increasing ferment among the peoples of Latin America, who want improved social conditions, educational facilities, health services, the comforts of modern living, and political stability. Repeatedly these people have been told that democracy can meet the challenge. Is the United States interested in the success of democracy in this vast neighboring area? Can the United States afford not to be interested? Can the United States disappoint the democratic groups who are waging a double fight against the totalitarianism of the left and the totalitarianism of the right?

. . . Anti-United States feeling, far more prevalent than communism, is largely due to disappointment. People do not understand why wars have been and are fought for democracy elsewhere under the guidance of the United States while their own democratic leaders are in prison or in exile without having recourse to any great power or a body of nations. . . .

I do not want to be impatient, knowing how steep the hill of human progress is. But the people are impatient. The people of Latin America have already heard enough of democracy and social justice, of the Organization of American States, and of the United Nations. They expect the large democratic powers, especially the United States, to exert their influence in the international organizations in order that those principles to which we have sworn allegiance may be enjoyed by all. The subject is not easy. The problems are not few. The burdens of United States officials are not light. But in due time democracy has to make itself felt as a guiding force in the development of the retarded nations of the West. A very definite popular feeling exists that democracy must meet the challenge of the times or fall into disrepute.

The main effort, of course, has to come from Latin America itself, from its democratic groups. But the weight of the United States is so overwhelming, its "intervention" so ever present by omission, that it is almost impossible for it not to influence the course of events one way or another. It is often pointed out that some mistakes have been made in trying to foster democracy which have brought about bad results. If so, the errors must have

been in the procedure, not in the policy. The good faith
cannot be questioned, and the policy should not be
discarded. Certainly, President Roosevelt's speeches expressing this country's moral support for democratic
government were an unforgettable encouragement. More
recently, it was an enlightened decision of the Eisenhower
administration to aid the revolutionary regime of Bolivia.
I wish the Bolivian revolution and the United States policy
toward it were better known. Here is proof, if it is
needed, that, disregarding doctrinary discrepancies, the
United States is sympathetic toward the political and social
progress of one of the poorest groups of people in Latin
America.

To preserve democracy in those countries where it has
been established—like Uruguay, Chile, or Costa Rica—
and to help to establish it in others, the United States
should exert its influence to the highest degree compatible
with diplomatic relations. I know very well the objections
raised to this idea in both Americas. I have heard those
objections dozens of times and I respect them, but I am
not convinced by them. There are at least two things that
the United States can do to foster democracy without
intervention. One is to discriminate in the realms of
diplomatic courtesies, and even . . . financing, in favor
of freely elected governments. The other is to make its
moral influence felt more strongly in the Organization of
American States.

— Reading No. 3 —

WHY VICE-PRESIDENT NIXON WAS SPAT UPON[3]

José Figueres, ex-President of Costa Rica, delivered this blunt statement before a Congressional Committee on June 9, 1958, following the unexpected outcome of Vice-President Nixon's trip to South America.

↗   ↗   ↗

As a citizen of the Hemisphere, as a man who has dedicated his public life to the cultivation of inter-American understanding, as a student who knows and esteems the United States, and who has never tried to conceal that esteem from anyone, no matter how hostile, I deplore the fact that the people of Latin America, as represented by a handful of over-excited Venezuelans, should have spit at a worthy functionary, who represents the greatest nation of our times. But I must speak frankly, even rudely, because I believe that the situation requires it: people cannot spit at a foreign policy, which is what they wanted to do. And when they have run out of other ways of making themselves understood, their only remaining recourse is to spit.

With all due respect for Vice President Nixon, and with all my admiration for his conduct, which was, during the events, heroic, and afterwards, noble, I must explain

[3] José Figueres, "No se puede escupir a una política exterior," *Combate,* No. 1 (July-August, 1958, San José, Costa Rica), pp. 64-66, *passim.* The statement Sr. Figueres made in Washington was also printed in the "Review of the Relations of the United States and other American Republics," *Hearings Before the Subcommittee on Inter-American Affairs of the Committee on Foreign Relations, House of Representatives, Eighty-fifth Congress, Second Session* (U.S. Government Printing Office, 1958), pp. 73-93.

that the act of spitting, vulgar though it is, is without
substitute in our language for expressing certain emotions. . . .

If you are going to talk about human dignity to Russia,
why is it so difficult to talk about the dignity of man to the
Dominican Republic? Which is intervention, which non-
intervention? Is it that a mere potential menace to your
own liberties is, essentially, more serious than the con-
summated rape of our liberties?

Of course, you have made certain investments in the
American dictatorships. The aluminum companies extract
bauxite almost gratis. Your generals, your admirals, your
civil functionaires, and your magnates receive royal treatment there. As your Senate verified yesterday, some con-
cessionaires bribe the reigning dynasties with millions for
the privilege of hunting on their grounds. They deduct the
money from the taxes they pay in the United States, but it
returns to the country, and upon arrival in Hollywood
is converted into extravagant furs and automobiles which
shatter the fragile virtue of the female stars.

Meanwhile, our women are raped by gangsters, our men
castrated in the torture chambers, and our illustrious
professors disappear lugubriously from the halls of
Columbia University in New York. When one of your
legislators calls this "collaboration to combat communism," 180 million Latin Americans want to spit.

Spitting is a despicable practice, when it is physically
performed. But what about moral spitting? When your
government invited Pedro Estrada, the Himmler of the
Western Hemisphere, to be honored in Washington, did
you not spit in the faces of all the democrats of America?

. . . I can assure you that, in international economic
policy, the United States gives the appearance of being
bent on repeating certain errors of the domestic policy
which did so much damage in the past, not excepting, of
course, those which led to the great crisis in 1929.

We Latin Americans are tired of pointing out these
mistakes, especially the lack of interest in the prices of
our products. Every time we suggest some plan to stabilize
prices at a just level, you answer us with slogans, with
such novelties as "the law of supply and demand," or
"the system of free interprise," or with insults as "Aren't
we giving you enough money now?"

We are not asking for hand-outs, except in cases of emergency. We are not people who would spit for money. We have inherited all the defects of the Spanish character, but also some of its virtues. Our poverty does not abate our pride. We have our dignity.

What we want is to be paid a just price for the sweat of our people, the sap of our soil, when we supply some needed product to another country. This would be enough for us to live, and to raise our own capital, and to pursue our own development.

— Reading No. 4 —

THE WEAKNESS OF PAN AMERICANISM[4]

Jorge Castañeda is an official of the Mexican Foreign office, but the following statement is not necessarily the official view of the Mexican government. Castañeda had the collaboration of a distinguished study group assembled at the Colegio de México. This statement is part of a book in a series sponsored by the Carnegie Endowment for International Peace.

✓　　　✓　　　✓

What is the regional "reality" of the American continent? How favorable are conditions in this continent for an authentic regional agency, both from a political and from an economic point of view? . . .

In its economic aspect, Pan Americanism has not even succeeded in establishing those basic principles of inter-

[4] Jorge Castañeda, "Pan Americanism and Regionalism: A Mexican View," *International Organization*, X (Boston, 1956), pp. 374-388, *passim*. Reprinted by permission.

American cooperation which might contribute positively
to raising the standard of living of the Latin American
peoples. The reason largely stems from the fact that the
Pan American organs and instruments, by their very
nature, do not reflect, nor are they based on, the real
division of the continent into two clearly differentiated
economic zones, which have fundamentally opposing
economic problems, interests, and aims, although their
economies are complementary. . . .

Those [political] principles which are most important in
the continent have not yet . . . formed bonds of solidarity sufficiently strong to create a political Pan
American community. Some, such as the non-recognition
of the validity of territorial conquest, the pacific settlement
of disputes, or the postulate of representative democracy
are common to the American peoples but not to them
exclusively. . . . Other important principles, like that of
non-intervention, have a negative character and their very
nature, origin and importance reveal the basic political
antagonism that divides the two Americas. . . .

The principle of common defense against outside
forces, which by its nature might contribute to the
strengthening American solidarity, has become a principle
which today presents serious risks for Latin America due
to the extra-continental political and military interests of
its North American associate. . . . Other principles, excellent in themselves, like the international protection of
democracy and human rights and the non-recognition
of dictatorships imposed by violence, have not been established in America for fear that they might be used as
instruments of intervention in the Latin American countries. . . .

The lack of continental political solidarity has been at
the same time cause and effect of the absence of a true Pan
American spirit. What has living reality in the conscience
of Latin American people is the feeling and the bonds of
Latin Americanism. . . . Important sectors of continental
public opinion still are convinced that the permanent
activity of Pan Americanism, centered in the Pan American Union and other principal bodies located in Washington, is too closely identified with the United States government, its policies and interests. . . . Pan Americanism has
existed for sixty years as a system and it still has not

succeeded in penetrating the conscience of our peoples. Except for some isolated incident during the Good Neighbor period, it would be difficult to verify during this long period any powerful and spontaneous public manifestation which would have lent it force and reality. . . .

The new grouping of political forces in the world has helped accentuate the artificial character of Pan Americanism.

— Reading No. 5 —

THE ORGANIZATION OF AMERICAN STATES: AN EXAMPLE FOR THE WORLD[5]

Alberto Lleras Camargo, now President of Colombia and one of the hemisphere's most respected statesmen, delivered an address under this title on April 29, 1954, at Bucknell University, as Secretary General of the Organization of American States. The first Latin American to hold this position, which had been monopolized in the past by U.S. citizens, he had served in this post since 1948 when the Pan American Union was transformed into the OAS and entrusted with additional responsibilities. He made a similar statement at Caracas on June 4, 1954, at the Tenth Pan American Conference.

Dr. Lleras Camargo spoke optimistically at Caracas, for he stated that economic problems of the hemisphere could be solved. He admitted that "millions of words, some pleasant, some wrathful and others persuasive, had to be exchanged via the channels of the Organization

[5] Lewisburg, Pennsylvania: Bucknell University Press, 1954, pp. 7-8, 15-16, *passim*. Reprinted by permission.

before essential agreements were reached that made it impossible to differ any longer on the first principles of Pan Americanism." [6]

ﾉ   ﾉ   ﾉ

The strongest and most deep-rooted of these prejudices is the notion that the American organization is the tool of North American imperialistic policy. Even among many of the citizens of this land such a thought is to be found, though perhaps expressed in other words. They believe in good faith that, in view of the material power and prestige of the United States, it would be very simple for it to adopt an inter-American policy that would permit it to exercise relative control over any situation that might arise in this hemisphere. The Russians, and most of the Europeans, have always subscribed to a similar belief. That is why they respond with such scornful incredulity when someone points to our organization as one to be emulated. When the Charter of the United Nations was being drawn up at San Francisco in 1945, and the Latin American states waged a victorious fight to preserve intact the system they and the United States had recently re-affirmed and strengthened at Chapultepec, the non-American countries could not get over their amazement. . . .

Every day, both in this country and abroad, we hear it said that the United States lacks experience in international affairs, lacks a definite foreign policy and good judgment in the management of its relations with other nations. The fact is, however, that in that section of the world in which the United States has had occasion to work out its international course over the longest period of time and under normal conditions, it has produced a genuine masterpiece. In its inter-American dealings are to be found intelligence and elasticity, self-control and tact, and the courage to promote great ideals without fear of the consequences. . . .

Even with its present imperfections, our Organization is the best experiment in international coexistence the world has ever tried. It was our Organization that first paved the way for the world associations of nations, and she who tutored those who were to propose for the entire

[6] Farewell address by Dr. Lleras at Caracas.

globe a new way of international life, that at first appeared to be one of the utopic dreams of ancient philosophers.

We owe it to our Organization that imperialism has not prospered in America, and surely her patient work over more than half a century of persuasion and vigilance against the threat of violence has done more for the independence of our young republics than have any tumultuous attacks on imperialism.

She has made the strong nations of America realize the necessary limitations of international action, and at the same time she has convinced the weaker ones of the tremendous power of mere words to keep in check, with their seemingly fragile barrier, armed arbitrariness and the threat of force.

She has developed the concept, through many years of effective co-operation among the members, that power must be shared by the nations if it is to endure, and that there is a duty, accompanied by an advantage, to extend and share the benefits that good fortune has heaped on one land and one group of people.

— Reading No. 6 —

LATIN AMERICA LOOKS TO CATHOLIC ACTION FOR A PROGRAM OF SOCIAL REFORM[7]

One of the most careful analyses of the present state of Latin America and what the church should do comes from

[7] Manuel Larraín, "Lo que espera de la Acción Católica la América Latina de hoy," *Revista Javeriana,* XLVII (Bogotá, June, 1957) No. 235, pp. 251-264, *passim.* Reprinted by permission.

the pen of Mons. Manuel Larraín, Bishop of Talca in Chile.

ꜰ   ꜰ   ꜰ

We find ourselves facing a situation which has two apparently paradoxical aspects: unity and separation in Latin America. Unity of historical and social background. Unity in its first evangelization and in its religious physiognomy. Unity of the many intellectual, ideological and social movements which are now going on in Latin America. But political and economic separation which strongly differentiate one nation from another. Division in apostolic action and, specifically, in the Catholic social action of the Church. . . .

In general terms we may describe the social physiognomy of Latin America as follows:

An aristocratic class which goes back to colonial times and which maintains up to the present the psychology of a ruling class. A plutocracy—which does not always coincide with the aristocracy—generally descended from European or Middle Eastern tradesmen who immigrated after the beginning of the republican era (second half of the nineteenth century to the present). The total absence through the nineteenth century and the beginning of the twentieth of a strong middle class comparable to the European *bourgeoisie*. The populace, the product of the intermingling of races, in a debased intellectual and economic situation. Great development of large land holdings and as a consequence a peasant class which has not come of age socially speaking. Add to this another social factor of decisive importance, common to all of Latin America: the weakness of the family as an institution. Without any attempt at statistical exactness, we can cite the high proportion of illegitimately born as a social fact common to all the Latin American nations. Various causes, also common, have brought about this situation: historically, the conquerors did not marry with the Indian women, so that the first fusion of the European with the indigenous races came about under the stigma of illegitimacy; ethnically, the tradition of polygamy among the greater part of the Indian tribes of America; socially, the fact that the European immigrant of the nineteenth century came generally without his family, and hence did not bring with him a strong family tradition (unlike the immigrants of the eighteenth century, who came with their families, whence a solid family tradition which still maintains itself); materially, an irregular way of life due to the lack of an economic basis sufficient to support settled family existence.

Finally, we must not forget the Indian problem of most Latin American nations, in many of which the Indian is only externally assimilated to western civilization. This, then, in broad outline, is the social situation of these countries. . . .

The Latin American republics came into being during a period which was especially difficult for the Church in Europe. It was the time of the triumphs of the liberal ideas of the encyclopaedists in the French Revolution. These ideas fired the men of the independence movement. Then came the most thriving period of Masonry in Europe with its anticlerical and naturalistic concepts. Next, after the mid-nineteenth century, came the rise of socialism.

All these ideas were allowed to operate powerfully on Latin America. All the American nations can tell the story of struggles, diverse in detail but identical in their basis.

What resistance did these ideas encounter from Catholic opinion? The twenty years following the achievement of independence, when the Church was almost without hierarchy, produced a great deal of confusion in the internal life of the Church in Latin America. The crisis of the seminaries brought about a decrease of the number of priests, which during the nineteenth century came to an extremely low ebb. Hence the advance of these ideas did not meet with sufficient resistance. Three areas reflect this situation: the fields of intellectual, social and political activity. I will speak only of the first two. . . .

Latin America is a continent on the verge of profound social reforms. The terrible social inequality already described, the great proletarian and subproletarian masses which live under inhuman conditions, the continued toleration of large land holdings united to a feudal regimen in rural areas, the lack of any sense of social responsibility among many of the Catholics who enjoy a comfortable economic condition, these are factors which bring home to us the urgency of taking a definite stand in this question of social reform. As His Excellency the Archbishop of

Manaos said at Manizales: "Social reform will come about, whether through our efforts or in spite of them. But in the latter case, it will be anti-Catholic. . . ."

This view of the matter implies a problem: in the new world which is rapidly coming into being, does Latin America have a decisive role to play? What will that role be? Will it be an atheistic, anticlerical, materialistic role? Or will it be a Christian role, constructive and charged with hopes? . . .

The social problem has assumed an extreme seriousness in Latin America for three reasons: (a) because of the enormous social differences, greater than those which exist on any other continent, (b) because of the subhuman situation of large groups within Latin American society (the peasants, Indians, and subproletarian masses), (c) because of the rapid technological evolution of the continent, which is progressing not by easy stages, but by dizzying leaps and bounds.

This situation is aggravated by the lack of strong traditions of family life, social cohesion, and respect for labor. The Church does not have sufficient influence in the field of organized labor. The great syndical movements do not reflect a decisive Catholic influence.

Social disquiet is becoming more and more acute.

The power of syndicalism is becoming almost omnipotent.

Neither in national nor international affairs is there the least sign of a plan for concerted action. Latin America, due to the inequitable distribution of its arable lands, due to the abuses which have arisen from this cause, and due to the material and social condition in which the peasant exists, is ripe for agricultural reform at a very near date, although this may vary from nation to nation (for example, Mexico and Bolivia). The nature and inspiration of this reform depends upon Catholic international action. . . .

OUR COLLABORATION WITH THE UNITED STATES

I believe it my duty to speak here, even though briefly, of an important point: our collaboration with the United States. (a) The economic, cultural and political influence of the United States in Latin America is obvious. (b) Protestant action in Latin America is largely inspired and financed in the United States. (c) The action of the Catholics of the United States in Latin America, although weak, has been proven possible and fruitful (e.g., the Maryknoll Missionaries). (d) A sentiment of distrust on our part toward the United States is mistaken, disadvantageous and un-Christian. (e) The ignorance concerning Latin America of the North American Catholics, including their vague judgments, may be partly their fault, but we are also guilty because we have not let ourselves be known as we really are. (f) Whereas commerce, cultural missions, students, radio and television increasingly link the United States with Latin America, the Catholics of North America and Latin America remain strangers, separated one from another. (g) Any projected international Latin American Catholic action should also take the Church of the United States into consideration. (h) Many prejudices must be overcome and a mutual effort to understand be made, past events forgotten, and with clear historical insight and above all the insight of the Church, the Catholicism of Latin America must be brought into closer communion with that of the United States. Each can confer many benefits upon the other. Both will profit and, above all, the Church will profit also.

— Reading No. 7 —

NEW WORLD, NEW RACES, AND NEW ART[8]

A persistent concern of Latin Americans has been the question of their cultural independence from Europe and their determination to make a distinctive and original

[8] *Textos de Orozco,* edited by Justino Fernández, Mexico City: Instituto de Investigaciones Estéticas, Universidad Nacional Autónoma de México, 1955, pp. 42-43. Reprinted by permission.

contribution based on New World conditions and needs. The Mexican painter José Clemente Orozco thought deeply on these matters.

✓   ✓   ✓

The art of the New World cannot take root in the old traditions of the Old World nor in the aboriginal traditions represented by the remains of our ancient Indian peoples. Although the art of all races and of all times has a common value—human, universal—each new cycle must work for itself, must create, must yield its own production, its individual share to the common good.

To go solicitously to Europe, bent on poking about its ruins in order to import them and servilely to copy them, is no greater error than is the looting of the indigenous remains of the New World with the object of copying with equal servility its ruins or its present folk-lore. However picturesque and interesting these may be, however productive and useful ethnology may find them, they cannot furnish a point of departure for the new creation. To lean upon the art of the aborigines, whether it be of antiquity or of the present day, is a sure indication of impotence and of cowardice, in fact, of fraud.

If *new* races have appeared upon the lands of the *New World,* such races have the unavoidable duty to produce a *New Art* in a new spiritual and physical medium. Any other road is plain cowardice. . . .

The highest, the most logical, the purest and strongest form of painting is the mural. In this form alone, is it one with the other arts—with all the others. It is, too, the most disinterested form, for it cannot be made a matter of private gain; it cannot be hidden away for the benefit of a certain privileged few.

It is for the people. It is for ALL.

RUSSIA, THE UNITED STATES, AND LATIN AMERICA[9]

Daniel Cosío Villegas has shown a notable catholicity of intellectual interests and capacities. Trained as a lawyer, he carried on advanced studies in economics in Europe and the United States, served as professor in various institutions of his country, Mexico, and represented it at numerous international conferences. Founder of the review El Trimestre Económico, *he also established and directed from 1934 to 1948 the Fondo de Cultura Económica, one of the most imaginative publishing houses in the hemisphere. In recent years, with the help of the Rockefeller Foundation, he has embarked upon a new career as historian, by organizing a group of younger scholars who have been producing with him an ambitious* Historia moderna de México *(4 vols., 1955-1958).*

✓ ✓ ✓

Today's world has two centers of gravity, Washington and Moscow, and because these centers are new, and because they are the only ones . . . today the world is going through a process of adjustment and readjustment. The Hispanic American countries cannot avoid taking part in this. . . . It is evident that the future international orbit of our countries will be determined in good part by our will and by our actual efforts to make a way for ourselves, and doubtless to an even greater extent, by the results of the contest between the United States and Russia. . . .

Often I have asked myself and others if we have anything to gain from the Soviet Union, and unfortunately

[9] Daniel Cosío Villegas, *Extremos de América,* Mexico: Tezontle, 1949, pp. 222-245, *passim.* Reprinted by permission.

I do not believe that I can answer this question except with a resounding negative. I say "unfortunately," because it seems to me that without a doubt the great pains which Russia takes to live to herself deprive the world . . . of some of the very few possibilities which the world has today for self-renovation and spiritual self-enrichment.

I suspect, in the first place, that Russia has few things to give us, and secondly, it seems certain that she has no mind to do so. What would you suggest that Russia might be able to give us? Money, for example? I doubt that she has it in such extreme abundance, for you must not forget that, on the one hand, the Soviet Union is a country whose economic, political, and social modernization has hardly begun and, on the other hand, that the war destroyed beyond repair much of what had been achieved. To this must be added the fact that Russia apparently considers a new global war inevitable, and therefore the principal object of her anxieties is to be prepared for this conflict. Thus if it is necessary to invest some money outside the country, she will do it without a doubt in countries which can protect her and aid her by their geography or affinity.

Would she give us, if necessary, political support? It is perfectly conceivable that Latin America could obtain the votes of Russia and her "satellites" if we called for them at some international conference in support of a proposal, particularly one unfavorable to the United States. . . .

Can we take advantage of the technical advances of Russia, of her artistic and educational innovations, that is, of her culture? Doubtless we would derive from this a sure and an immense profit; but it is also true that there seems for the time being to exist no real possibility of this happening: the Soviet Union propagates the notion abroad that it is a beehive of art, of science, of technology; but little is done to demonstrate this, still less to share it. . . .

Unlike Russia, from which we have little or nothing to expect, the United States can give us everything, or almost everything: money, technical aid, and political and military protection. From the point of view of advantage, then, no responsible person can doubt the attraction of the United States for us. But there is more than the attraction of advantage . . . ; there is also geographic fate and what we might call historical coincidence. The first lies in the obvious fact that we live on the same continent; . . . By "historical coincidence" I mean simply that, like the United States, we are branches—it does not matter how underdeveloped or secondary—of the great tree of Western Civilization. Therefore, our general way of life is much more like that of the Yankee than that of, let us say, the Russian. This is a bond much stronger than one might suppose; for me it is as important as the economic, and hardly less cogent than the geographic. . . .

The United States, then, can give Hispanic America everything, or almost everything; but in exchange for money and subjection. Yet we must not forget . . . that the geographic circumstance of our living on one continent and the historical coincidence of our similar ways of life also make for subjection. . . .

And now let us turn to the final aspect of our theme: the attitude of Hispanic America in face of a possible conflict between the United States and Russia . . .

To think that in this conflict we could be against the United States seems to me not only impossible, but unjustifiable, at least not unless that country should offend us in some irreparable way or become converted to political ideas mutually exclusive with our own convictions concerning liberty and democracy; but I believe that the solutions which it is fruitful to investigate are those which presuppose that such a conflict will not occur, or that if it occurs, we will be neither on the side of the United States nor against them. The two solutions are, in fact, one and the same, for one of the few ways in which the war can be avoided would be by an inequivocal and early declaration on the part of the Latin American nations (and China and India also), announcing, first, that they do not believe war between the United States and Russia to be either necessary or justified; second, that if it happens, they will take no part in it.

— Reading No. 9 —

RECIPROCITY AND MUTUAL RESPECT ARE ESSENTIAL[10]

Brazil is a continent, and Brazilians think in continental terms. Here a Brazilian social historian and statesman, Gilberto Freyre, speaks for all Latin America.

✓　　　　✓　　　　✓

Reciprocity and mutual respect seem to me an essential basis for developing really friendly inter-American relations. This mutual respect should take into consideration the fact that a democratic tradition is common to all Americans, Latin and Anglo-Saxon. The Latins have developed the ethnic aspect of democracy more than the political, and the Anglo-Saxons the purely political aspect more than the ethnic. If they are to become really good neighbors and increasingly democratic in their organizations and culture, Latin and Anglo-Saxon Americans will probably enrich each other with the best results of their special culture developments. But it would be a sociological error to work for uniformity in the American hemisphere instead of for unity combined with variety—though the respect for variety should not go so far as to include tolerance of such undemocratic institutions as *caudillismo* or lynching, anti-Semitism, and the Ku Klux Klan. . . .

As the Second World War made clear that the United States would emerge as the great imperial super-power of a new phase in the history of capitalism, fear of "Yankee" financial and industrial lords began to increase among Latin Americans. Latin American nations should

[10] Gilberto Freyre, *New World in the Tropics,* New York: Alfred A. Knopf, 1959, pp. 186-187, 272-273. Reprinted by permission.

concentrate their nationalism in economic issues instead of satisfying themselves with mere political appearances of independence. Hence, the numerous Latin American restrictions and measures put into effect since the thirties and intensified after the end of the Second World War, measures against exploitation of mines and water power by foreigners; against the establishment of deposit banks and insurance companies with shares held by foreigners; against the ownership by foreigners not only of agricultural land (until the foreigners have established permanent residence as farmers), but also of enterprises considered national in their purposes; of restrictions even against the practice by foreigners of liberal professions . . .

Similar measures have been taken in Latin America during the last decades to protect native labor against foreign intrusion, a typical law specifying that foreigners shall not constitute more than one-third of the employees or receive more than one-third of the wages or salary of any industrial, commercial, or public-utility enterprise except in certain industries. Besides this, measures have been taken against foreign intrusion, to favor so-called industrialization programs, making them expressions of an intensive economic nationalism. Privileges of almost sacred value have been claimed by industrialists and patriots during recent decades . . . for domestic manufactures as opposed to imported commodities that once were exalted as angelic marvels and are now considered diabolical when imported from the United States. Through their influence in the press, industrialists have been able to create in some parts of Latin America a sort of industrialist *mystique* or fad that has meant, in more than one case, the neglect of agriculture—for agriculture should be left to colonial peoples—and, almost always, hostility toward the United States, now the only super-industrial power whose influence is seen as an immediate "danger" by economic nationalists in some Latin American areas.

— Reading No. 10 —

SOME LATIN AMERICAN LEADERS DON'T WANT TECHNOLOGICAL CHANGE[11]

Loans are not enough to improve economic conditions in Latin America. Ideas are involved, too, if any useful directed culture change is to be achieved. An American political scientist, William S. Stokes of Claremont Men's College, here advances the provocative thesis that the change will not come until the Latin American intellectuals (Pensadores) *accept the ideas on which modern technology is based.*

✓　　　　✓　　　　✓

Hispanic culture has long been characterized by the belief that leisure ennobles and labor, especially technical labor, degrades. Indeed, this psychological attitude toward production probably explains better than any other single factor why the Latin American countries are, in varying degrees, backward in the material sense. The values in Hispanic culture with respect to work and leisure have a direct and important relationship to technical assistance aid programs of the United States. . . .

It follows logically from the general principle that work is debasing, leisure ennobling, that the highest status is accorded those who live in ostentation without labor of any kind. . . . Some of such high status professions are: top level bureaucrat, lawyer, doctor, poet, priest, general. Government employment is sought most seriously. To be

[11] William S. Stokes, "The Drag of the Pensadores," in James W. Wiggins and Helmut Schoeck, eds., *Foreign Aid Reexamined*, Washington, D.C.: Public Affairs Press 1958, pp. 76, 79, 56-57, 62-63, 68. Reprinted by permission.

a high level bureaucrat is to enjoy high status. A sinecure is best of all lower-level positions. It is widely believed throughout Latin America that secondary education permits the individual to consider himself privileged never to work with his hands. . . .

The wealthy, talented, educated, cultured, traveled upper-middle classes which govern everywhere in Latin America have never been denied the knowledge of technology. The libraries, book stores, and repositories of the United States Government Printing Office are packed with millions of items on health, sanitation, education, agriculture, industry, commerce, manufacturing, banking, accounting, statistics, business management, public administration and the like. Latin Americans are free to visit the United States any time to observe how we farm or manufacture or carry on administration. Institutions of higher learning are ready to accept graduate students. Professors are ready to impart knowledge of their specialties to the best of their ability. In fact, it is fair to say that the United States has always been willing to share ideas and experiences for the asking.

However, the evidence indicates that the leaders of Latin America never have done much asking. Probably no peoples on earth live more graciously and serenely than the elites which govern in Latin America. On the other hand, even in the most advanced countries such as Argentina, Chile, Uruguay, Brazil, Cuba and Costa Rica, it is evident even to the casual observer that the masses of the people live poorly. . . .

If those people with maximum status, dignity, power and influence in Latin American society have not seen fit to spend their time and money in studying science, technology, and administration for adaptation to their own cultures, what are the reasons for their failure to do so? The hypothesis of this paper is that they have chosen not to do so because the values of Hispanic culture are in conflict with the values of modern-day technology. Consciously or unconsciously they prefer the values of their own culture and hence resist change. . . .

The unavailability of education for the masses, lack of equality of economic opportunity, authoritarianism in various of the social institutions, and tradition help to explain the existence and perpetuation of a rigid class system in most of the Latin American countries. Among those with status, dignity and influence in the community, few rank higher in the continuum than the *pensadores* or intellectuals—the poets, novelists, essayists, artists, and professional people. . . . They have almost unanimously expressed the conviction that the values of Hispanic and Anglo-American culture are in conflict. More than that, the central theme in the thinking of the great majority of the intellectuals is the . . . superiority of the values of Hispanic culture and the inferiority of the values of United States culture. . . .

It is clear that the *pensadores* do not accept and advance the values of technology and technological change represented by the kind of technical assistance and economic aid the United States has made available in the past and apparently will make available in larger amounts in the future. The fact that the *pensadores* either ignore technology, accept it grudgingly and with many misgivings, or outright oppose it means that they are an obstacle to the development of a successful foreign aid program in Latin America.

— Reading No. 11 —

RUBÉN DARÍO (1867-1916): TO ROOSEVELT[12]

The Darío influence over the poets of Spanish America has waned since his death in 1916. Yet the attitude expressed by Darío in his ode to Theodore Roosevelt is still found far and wide below the Rio Grande.

✓　　　　　✓　　　　　✓

[12] Thomas Walsh, ed., *Hispanic Anthology,* New York: Hispanic Society of America, 1920, pp. 597-598. Adapted from the translation by Elijah Clarence Hills. Reprinted by permission.

The United States are rich, they're powerful and great
(They join the cult of Mammon to that of Hercules),
And when they stir and roar, the very Andes shake . . .
But our America, which since the ancient time . . .
Has had its native poets; which lives on fire and light,
On perfumes and on love; our vast America
The land of Montezuma, the Inca's mighty realm,
Of Christopher Columbus the fair America,
America the Spanish, the Roman Catholic, . . .
O men of Saxon eyes and fierce, barbaric soul,
This land still lives and dreams, and loves and stirs!
   Take care!
The daughter of the Sun, the Spanish land, doth lives!
And from the Spanish lion a thousand whelps have sprung!
'Tis need, O Roosevelt, that you be God himself,
The fear-inspiring Rifler and Champion of the chase,
If you would hold us in your grasping, iron claws.
With all that you possess, one thing is lacking:
   God!

— Reading No. 12 —

UNDERNOURISHED LATIN AMERICA[13]

Most population experts look at the future darkly, as do Mr. Brown in this reading and such Latin American writers as Josué de Castro in The Geography of Hunger *(Boston: Little, Brown & Co., 1952). Other authorities such as M. K. Bennett, of the Food Research Institute of*

[13] Harrison Brown, "Life in the Americas During the Next Century," *Annals of the American Academy of Political and Social Science,* vol. 316 (March, 1956), pp. 13-16, *passim.* Reprinted by permission.

Stanford University, in his The World's Food (*New York: Harper Brothers, 1954*) *feel that some of these black clouds are blown up by interested parties to make our flesh creep with a view to stimulating support for action.*

✓   ✓   ✓

The greater part of Latin America is undernourished today. In the main the situation in most regions is not at present as critical as it is in the greater part of Asia, but diets are sub-standard and roughly equivalent in caloric value to the average diets in most of Southern Europe and the Near East. The average daily caloric intake is about 2,400 and varies from about 1,900 in Peru to 3,200 in Argentina.

Most of the terrain is highly subject to erosion. Further, the destructive agricultural and forestry practices to which many regions are now being exposed are resulting in serious soil depletion coupled with an actual decrease in the carrying capacity of the land. In principle this degradation can be stopped, and vast areas of land can be put under cultivation. But in order to do this the most advanced technology must be applied on a tremendous scale. Much research is needed before the major problems of tropical agriculture can really be solved. And the solutions, when found, will undoubtedly require the attainment of substantial levels of industrialization, the investment of considerable capital, and the adoption of these new and advanced techniques by the greater part of the population. . . .

But many regions of Latin America are not blessed with adequate resources either to feed themselves or to provide for their own internal industrial development, let alone being able to trade resource surpluses in order to accumulate capital. Indeed from this point of view, and with the possible exceptions of Venezuela and Brazil, it appears that Latin America is considerably worse off than is India with respect to long-range development.

In addition there are serious shortages of energy resources in large areas of the region. There are fair reserves of available water power which can be important in accelerating the industrialization process, but which are negligible when compared with long-range power needs. There is apparently no coal of any real consequence.

There are substantial reserves of petroleum, but by the time the residents of Latin America are in a position to utilize liquid fuels on a large scale themselves, the reserves will long since have been transported in tankers to North America and to Europe. . . .

In the absence of major help from the outside it seems likely that, although industrial development in Latin America will proceed slowly, it will proceed more rapidly than agricultural development. If industrial development is sufficiently rapid, we can expect to see a retardation of the present rate of degradation of the land, followed by a gradual extension of agricultural area. But unless human fertility decreases fairly rapidly . . . it is doubtful that the lot of the average person in Latin America will improve appreciably during the course of the next century. . . . There will be considerable differences between areas, but the region as a whole seems destined to be an impoverished one far into the future. . . .

Clearly the process of development would be greatly speeded if considerable financial and technical help were to be given by the presently industrialized regions of the world. But there is little evidence that such help will be forthcoming in the future on a scale commensurate with the real need.

POPULATION PROBLEMS IN MEXICO AND CENTRAL AMERICA[14]

Population growth in the Central American region (including Mexico) has been very rapid in the recent past. Within the past 30 years, the population of Mexico has increased by more than three-quarters while that of Central America proper nearly doubled. In fact, this region has perhaps experienced the most rapid population growth of any region in the world. . . .

It is reasonable to expect that population will again grow rapidly in the coming 30 years. Growth will be further speeded up by the continued fall in death rates and only after a fall in birth rates . . . which can hardly be expected to occur before 1980, is there any prospect of slower growth. The population of Central America and Mexico will most probably continue to be among the fastest growing in the world. . . . Such rapid population growth will undoubtedly enhance the position which these countries occupy in world affairs. Whether it will be beneficial to the peoples concerned, however, depends also on many other considerations; it will require changes in outlook as regards internal policies for the economic development and cultural advancement of these countries . . .

The most important aspect of the number of inhabitants is its relation to the surface of the land. . . . With the exception of El Salvador, none of the countries are densely inhabited at the present time. . . . Population is very unevenly distributed within the countries of Central

[14] United Nations, *The Population of Central America (Including Mexico), 1950-1980,* Report I, Population Studies, No. 16, New York, 1954, pp. 11-23, *passim.* Reprinted by permission.

America and Mexico. High population densities exist, for example, in Central Mexico, in the highlands of Guatemala, on the central plateau of Costa Rica, and in the vicinity of the Canal Zone in Panama, while the large portions of the same countries are still very sparsely settled. The reasons for this uneven distribution of human settlement are partly topographic, partly climatic, and partly historical.

The rapid growth of population will . . . probably give rise to various schemes designed to encourage the resettlement of parts of the population . . . There will therefore be an ever-increasing need for further research, in the technological and geographical fields, to explore new economic opportunities as well as in the sociological and anthropological field to examine the motivations which often prevent people from fully availing themselves of existing opportunities.

The prosperity of most of Central America and certain parts of Mexico depends, at the present time, to a large measure on international trade with countries outside this region. Among the important items for export are coffee and bananas, of which the United States has become the chief consumer. A continued rise in the demand for such products abroad has, up to the present, been of greatest importance in the maintenance of balances of foreign trade because the needs for imported goods in these countries have also been growing rapidly. As the populations of Mexico and Central America continue to grow, so their needs for the goods which cannot be readily procured locally will also multiply. Because population in Central America will probably grow more rapidly than in the United States and many other parts of the world, there is some doubt whether the demand for Central American staple exports will continue to rise as rapidly as the local need for imported products. . . .

The continued large proportion of children and adolescents . . . gives rise to serious problems. In many areas of Central America (including Mexico), existing facilities for general popular education are not yet fully adequate to meet the needs of the present child population. It is true that great efforts are being made to extend general education to larger and larger segments of the population. Nevertheless, even these efforts will have to be further increased in the future if the needs of an ever-increasing child population are to be met. . . . A large proportion of children, furthermore, complicates the problem of economic development. . . . Economic and technological development . . . could probably be more rapid if fewer children depended on the given number of persons capable of contributing effectively to the output of goods and services.

— Reading No. 14 —

"A NEW CONCEPT OF INTERNATIONAL COOPERATION"[15]

An economics professor who has led the Socialist Party in Colombia, Antonio García represents a new viewpoint in Latin America. Neither pro-United States nor subservient to the Soviet party line, Sr. García believes that Latin America needs to employ efficiently its own resources rather than insist that a flood of dollars is necessary for its salvation.

✓   ✓   ✓

The area of our doctrinary freedom is necessarily delimited by two extreme currents. The one denies as a matter of principle the existence of any form of international cooperation—in the orbit of capitalism—and the other sees in international cooperation the magical remedy for all ills. The first is the current fed by the universal dogmata of communism, which deny to world organiza-

[15] Antonio García, *La rebelión de los pueblos débiles,* La Paz, Bolivia: Editorial "Juventud," 1955, pp. 129-132, *passim,* Reprinted by permission.

tions all capacity for cooperation and which counsel the backward nations nothing other than the most negative policy of resentment: the policy of not investing, of not importing capital, of not applying for Point Four aid, of not employing regional systems in order to obtain certain types of resources. Of course, this policy of negation as a matter of principle can be explained from the Russian point of view . . . but it cannot be justified from the point of view of the weak nations. It is sufficient to cite the example of Western Europe, where the Communists bitterly attacked the Marshall Plan—inasmuch as this plan was something of a program to rearm and reinforce the military preparedness of the western nations against the U.S.S.R.—but they understood that without the Marshall Plan dollars post-war economic rehabilitation would not have taken place. . . . The second is the "traditionalist" current . . . which believes frankly that all the problems . . . in backward nations can be resolved by means of international financial and technical cooperation. For example, our own country set off on the "Currie adventure" which can be cited as one of the most costly frauds ever perpetrated in the name of the desire of an underdeveloped country for planned development. The "Currie adventure" was built on the illusion that, once a Report . . . was drawn up, a river of dollars would gush forth from the World Bank . . . to provide the necessary financial nourishment. . . . The United States have in their hands the responsibility for the capitalistic world, but they have no obligation to finance anybody's industrialization. . . . Their criterion is not to fight against Communism by seeking practical ways to raise underdeveloped economies and eliminate all reasons for resentment: ignorance, chronic poverty, fear. The United States believe that it is possible to fight Communism with merely political and military means. We may well think that such a policy is based upon a most dangerous illusion, but that illusion is the guiding factor of the financial policy of the United States. . . . Our strategy should not be a strategy of complaint, as if the problem were simply a matter of moving the hearts of the Yankee bankers: our strategy should be one of efficient, complete, and correct utilization of the dollars which we receive. . . . The vital thing is not that we should receive

a larger dose of dollars, but that we should learn to invest them better: that is, that a new and realistic conception of the true possibilities of international cooperation
be followed by a new policy for the adequate utilization
of those possibilities.

— Reading No. 15 —

IF I WERE A DICTATOR[16]

*Under this title the late Chester Lloyd Jones of the
University of Wisconsin wrote a penetrating and balanced
analysis of dictatorship in Latin America. Although he
writes about Guatemala, some of his remarks apply to
other countries of Latin America.*

✦   ✦   ✦

Dictators as a rule do not rule cowed peoples but those
who tolerate and even approve of their acts. . . .

The Spanish concept of liberty itself is often an ally of
dictatorship. No people are more jealous of individual
rights than are Spaniards. Those who have been shaped
by Spanish political ideals share this outstanding characteristic. The sectionalism which has been and still is characteristic of the mother country has sprung from the resistance of the Spaniard to forces which would press him
into a common mold. In spite of his enthusiasm for leaders who can shape men to their wills he stands as one
of the world's best examples of individualism. The in-
ability to reconcile the conflict between the desire for
freedom of individual expression and the longing for good
government, especially good administration, largely explains the Spanish shortcomings in the larger political

[16] Chester Lloyd Jones, *Guatemala Past and Present,* Minneapolis: The University of Minnesota Press, 1940, pp.
   339-356, *passim.* Reprinted by permission.

developments both in the Old World and the New. . . .

In the long run the better maintenance of order, better transportation, better health conditions, and better education may bring a social revolution in Guatemalan conditions by both incorporating the Indian in the active citizenry and increasing the opportunities open to the ladino. . . .

When these things are won, or as they are won, there may arise a greater interest in public affairs. The neighborhood horizon which limits the economic and social activities of so large a part of the population will be broadened. Public interest in public affairs will be stimulated and bring more intelligent participation in them. Only by some such steps of progress can it be expected that popular control of government such as obtains in more advanced democracies may arise. . . .

[No dictatorship] has escaped charges of violation of constitutional standards and of being guilty of heinous abuses. While these are regularly reported by the enemies of those in power and reach wide currency as a rule only after their alleged perpetrators are out of office or dead, they are so great in number and so often attested by such credible witnesses that their existence cannot be questioned. Assassinations having all the characteristics of murder, executions without trial or after trial before controlled courts, torture of political opponents and their relatives, the driving of political rivals into exile, and all manner of violations of person and property are reported in such number against both the earlier and more recent dictators that any unqualified defense of dictatorship as an institution of government in Guatemala is impossible. . . .

Whether the public programs which have been followed and the extragovernmental changes in the interests of the Guatemalan people will build the bridge between dictatorship and popular government no one can say. If they do develop the national wealth, raise the standard of life, bring the Indian into the currents of the modern world, increase the income of the national treasury to be used for the common good, diversify the ambitions of the citizenship, and create a well-knit Guatemalan nationality, dictators may decline in power as the people insist on taking a greater measure of authority into their own hands. But developments may be irregular and of unexpected consequence. . . .

If the Indian population continues to play no real role in public affairs a higher standard of life for it, if it comes, may still leave the state divided against itself. Perhaps too the Indian peoples may prove less politically able than some of their friends believe.

Economic crises which affect so deeply and so frequently the prosperity of monoculture countries may continue to upset the economic bases of the national life and thereby delay the winning of political stability. . . .

No one knows the formula for progress from dictatorship to popular government. How often have dictators been forced from power by democratic movements, with the result that order with sacrifice of liberty has been replaced by political chaos with no better guarantee of citizens' rights! How often, too, have hopes been aroused that dictators will show the necessary strength of character and the patriotism to permit the gradual lessening of their powers by peaceful means and how often have such hopes proved vain!

Neither the rulers nor the people of Guatemala can place all the blame upon the other for the failure to achieve that degree of popular government to which all profess to aspire. . . .

If Guatemala is to become a democracy in fact as well as in name, all factions must be willing to support governments which may gradually become more popular through a slow process of trial, error, and sacrifice. A survey of the experience of the republic does not indicate that such advance will be rapid, sustained, or free from disappointments. . . .

THE STRUCTURAL WEAKNESSES AND THE POTENTIAL OF NICARAGUA'S ECONOMY[17]

The International Bank for Reconstruction and Development sent a mission to study Nicaragua's economic needs and possibilities at the request of General Somoza. The mission returned to Washington in May, 1952, with a detailed report, whose conclusions are given below.

✓   ✓   ✓

From its nearly year-long travel in the country, the mission concluded that few underdeveloped countries have so great a physical potential for growth and economic development as does Nicaragua. In area this is the largest country in Central America. In relation to its present population, it has almost unlimited land for development. The land can grow nearly every tropical crop and many non-tropical crops.

By making effective use of its land resources, the country can become, in the future, an important exporter of meat and dairy products and of a diversified list of other agricultural products. It should continue as a producer of timber and minerals. It should develop a sound and well-balanced relationship between industry and agriculture.

The population of the country is a little over a million and, in contrast to its land, its manpower resources are relatively small. Compared with many underdeveloped countries the ratio of manpower to land is favorable. Though this small ratio of labor to land will impose man-

---

[17] *The Economic Development of Nicaragua,* Baltimore: Johns Hopkins Press, 1953, pp. 3-4. Reprinted by permission.

power shortages, the use of modern industrial and agricultural techniques can offset this handicap.

The physical resources of the country provide a sound basis for economic development. The variety, quality and extent of these resources are assessed in the technical sections of this report.

Nicaragua has many of the social, economic and governmental weaknesses typical of underdeveloped countries. Its Government is keenly aware of this.

The principal weak points in the past have been: (a) generally low standards of health and education; (b) an archaic fiscal system inadequate to advance the country's economic development and to encourage rising standards of living; (c) a transportation system improved in recent years but still inadequate; (d) an ineffective credit system, especially for the provision of medium and long-term agricultural and industrial credits; (e) an absence of long-range planning, and of a concrete investment program and policy coordination within the government; (f) a system of public administration requiring a general overhaul to carry out a development program.

Many of the weaknesses in the economic structure have been accentuated by conditions peculiar to the country. Though its people are notably cheerful and high spirited, they have had an unhappy and depressing history. There have been many civil wars in the past. These have been frequently accompanied by foreign intervention in the nation's political affairs. During the civil war of the 1920's there was direct foreign military intervention. The restoration of peace was followed by a major earthquake which destroyed the capital city. The economic depression of the 1930's seriously disrupted the export trade of the country. World War II brought fewer economic benefits to Nicaragua than to many Latin American countries.

This long history, together with the general backwardness and poverty of the country, discouraged economic progress and the establishment of a sound administrative and fiscal structure in the country.

— Reading No. 17 —

LAND USAGE IN EL SALVADOR[18]

Cuscatlán (Indian name for "El Salvador") meaning "land of abundance" is becoming less deserving of the name. . . . Only on a small part of the land—the 5 per cent under coffee cultivation—are adequate or semiadequate conservation practices being employed. On the balance of the land the methods of cultivation used are exhausting the soil in one way or another, in the great majority of cases . . . there is only one hectare of land for each Salvadorian, of which 8 per cent is arable land, 3 per cent is flooded land, 46 per cent is fairly fertile, but not level, land, and the balance produces very little.

From this one hectare of land, the Salvadorian is able to produce approximately some 100 colons ($40 U.S. currency) per year. . . . It should surprise no one that 80 per cent of the population of El Salvador are suffering from malnutrition. . . . In El Salvador natural resources are diminishing and the population increasing. . . . Each new increase in population means a greater demand on resources, with an acceleration in losses, and the problem of education becomes increasingly difficult to solve.

[18] Mario Pacheco and Alfredo Martínez, "Population of El Salvador and Its Natural Resources," *Proceedings of the Inter-American Conference on Conservation of Renewable Natural Resources, Denver, Colorado, September 7-20, 1948* (Washington, D.C. [1949]). pp. 129-132, *passim*. Reprinted by permission.

POLITICAL POWER IN HONDURAS[19]

Frequently violence has led to political power in Honduras, and unrestrained executive authority sanctioned by force has been more the rule than the exception. However the subject of government is examined, by the microscope or the telescope, the result is the same. Government in action is government by *caudillo, él que manda* (the one who commands), the military man on horseback, the *doctor en filosofía* from the lecture hall. The average Honduran knows that wherever government is able to operate the final authority is the executive.

In the administrative branch, in the legislature, in the administration of justice, and in departmental and local politics—everywhere, the hand of the executive can be seen. The structure is hierarchical; the working principle, authoritarian. It would be presumptuous to assign the origin of this system to any one source. One would have to consider a large number of geographical and cultural factors; but in large measure the system is the product of Spanish schooling in social, economic, and political authoritarianism for over 300 years. The institutions of the family, church, and army were largely authoritarian, and the political institution of monarchy fostered a feudal economic system.

Nevertheless, however paradoxical it may seem, the average Honduran is to a large extent a free agent, possessing the liberty to organize his household, operate his business, dispose of his property, and pursue his pleasures without great governmental regulation or control. It is therefore only within the sphere of a relatively small number of functions which the government performs that

[19] William S. Stokes, *Honduras, An Area Study in Government*, Madison: University of Wisconsin Press, 1950, pp. 294-300, *passim*. Reprinted by permission.

the executive's influence is absolute, or nearly so. These functions are mainly police, education, health, sanitation, and adjudication. . . .

If it can be demonstrated that the citizen enjoys considerable freedom in economic and social fields why should not one decide that the Honduran political system is highly desirable, and that it should be protected and perpetuated? The reasons are (1) that authority without responsibility has encouraged repudiation of government through revolution, a primitive expression of dissatisfaction which is socially undesirable; (2) that there is no incentive for the development of service functions through government; and (3) that the precedent of authoritarianism within a narrowly outlined sphere of activity is a dangerous stepping stone to totalitarianism.

Hondurans have repeatedly expressed dissatisfaction with their political system through revolutions, yet they have frequently said: "Our revolutions are not against principles but men." It is true that there has been general acceptance of the basic principles of the liberal democratic state since the 1880's—that is, government by the majority, protection of minority rights through equality before the law, and the welfare concept of utilitarianism. Yet Hondurans have failed to develop governmental institutions through which power can be popularly mobilized, held responsible, and changed periodically by honest and peaceful elections. For practical purposes, therefore, the "principles" represent at best long-term objectives, at worst, window-dressing for dictatorship. . . .

One cannot leave the field of research in Honduran government and politics with completely negative results. Indeed there is much to praise in both the theory and the actual working of government, which offers encouragement for even more favorable developments in the future. Racially homogeneous, nationalistic, with an economic system based on widespread ownership of land, Hondurans have a deep, almost profound appreciation of the dignity of man. Liberal democratic principles incorporated in all the modern constitutions have at least a symbolic value. The absence of a self-perpetuating social aristocracy, the fluidity and flexibility in the social classes, the large measure of equality of opportunity, all these point to considerable social and economic democracy. It is not

inconceivable that the principles of political democracy,
already widely accepted, will gradually be implemented.
One must not forget that there has been a reasonably
satisfactory beginning of a two-party system, in which
the political parties are based more on principle and program than on *personalismo;* that the national elections
of 1923, 1928, and 1932 were fair; that there is at least
the birth of that spirit of sportsmanship in accepting defeat which is indispensable to the democratic process.

— Reading No. 19 —

PANAMA: THE "GRINGO" AND
THE "SPIG":
MORALS AND MORES[20]

*Panamanians and U.S. citizens alike tend to consider
the Canal as the great fact of their relationship. Yet a
deeper conflict exists, according to the sociologists—a
difference in culture patterns here described. To appreciate fully these differences, a historical perspective is·
necessary. The prevalence of the mistress in Panamanian
society of all levels, for example—a situation to be found
to some extent throughout most of Latin America—cannot be understood without taking into account the facts
of the Spanish and Portuguese conquests of America in
which few European women participated and the conquerors took their mates from the subject races.*

*This is a subject on which much remains to be said.
When Latin Americans look at divorce statistics in the
United States, they conclude that we have little family
life and that we are a promiscuous people.*

✓   ✓   ✓

With caste differences placing the American in a su-

[20] John and Mavis Biesanz, *The People of Panama*, New York:
    Columbia University Press, 1955, pp. 178-181, 298-300,
    passim. Reprinted by permission.

perior position over the native Panamanians lumped with
other non-Americans below, with Americans acting as if
the Zone were their particular private preserve and Panamanians smarting under wounds to their sovereignty, one
could hardly expect close and harmonious relations between persons of the two nations. Add to this the language barrier, differences in customs, the economic self-
interest of each group, the contrasts in political systems,
economic organization, levels of living, and racial com-
position of the two groups, and we can see that resentments, frictions, and conflicts are inevitable.

The Canal-digger of construction days worked under
conditions which made home seem like "God's country,"
a feeling which he expressed in no uncertain terms. He
had little but contempt for the "natives" who lived in such
filth and disease, who did not speak his language, who
were not of his race, whose moral code was different,
who took life as easily as possible. They were different;
therefore they were inferior. . . .

By the time the Canal was finished, the Zone had become quite a comfortable and attractive place to live, and
the Americans wanted to stay and keep the best jobs for
themselves. The old-timers took great pride in their accomplishment; it was *their* Canal and *their* Zone. Through
the years they and their children, with a trickle of new
recruits who came in slowly enough to be incorporated
into Zone ways with little trouble, built up a self-sufficient
community which depended on Panama for little except
menial labor. Few Zonians met any Panamanians except
maids, lottery vendors, perhaps a few silver workers. After
decades there, many of them did not even know how to
ask for a bottle of beer at the beer garden in adequate
Spanish. The majority were utterly indifferent to and
ignorant of the language, the customs, and the beliefs of
their neighbors. Many accepted the stereotyped notion
that a "spig" was an ignorant, lazy "nigger" who was
none too clean, ungrateful for all that the United States
had done for him, a gambler, a person of loose morals,
a chiseler who thought the world, and most especially
Uncle Sam, owed him a living. The Zonian thought he
had assumed a fair share of "the white man's burden,"
for where would Panama be without the Americans? Still
savage, backward, unsanitated. . . .

Except for the few Zonians they met when they ventured across the street to ask for a job, most Panamanians saw Americans only as the roistering soldiers and sailors who occasionally figured in lurid episodes, or as wealthy tourists or businessmen who kept to their own crowd. Given these limited contacts and humiliating experiences, they could hardly form a rosy picture of their "good neighbor." Stereotypes typically take form when one contrasts the ideal behavior of one's own kind with the worst behavior of the other group. The gringo was conceived of as an immature, cocky, swaggering blond who considered himself superior to anyone else, especially to those with any Negro blood, and who enjoyed himself in foolish, rowdy ways. He was "money mad" and had no "culture." His women were loose. His nation was the Colossus of the North, run by imperialist bankers in Wall Street.

From the twenties on, the tide of nationalism rose steadily. Panamanians tried to stem the tide of Americanization. "Speak Spanish and count in balboas," reiterated Arnulfo Arias's *Acción Comunal*. They fostered pride in folk culture. They hotly defended "national sovereignty and territorial integrity" against "Yankee imperialism." They worked up a fever of resentment that simmered down only temporarily during the early years of the "good neighbor" policy, and then burned hotter than ever after the war, finally exploding in the rejection of the bases treaty in 1947.

La querida—the mistress—is found on all social levels, from the policeman or Zone laborer who tries to support two or three women and their children to the aristocrat who proves his masculinity by eloping with every lower-class Queen of the Carnival who proves willing.

The traditional seclusion of upper-class girls until marriage, the unbridled liberty of their brothers, and the existence of a large underprivileged group have made the *casa chica* (little house) a widespread institution in Latin America. In colonial Panama, men . . . went . . . in search of premarital and extramarital adventure. Many of them recognized their illegitimate children and thus gave rise to the large number of lower-class families who bear the same surnames as the aristocracy. Marriage was traditionally arranged to suit the parents' convenience;

romance was found elsewhere if it did not happen to coincide with marriage. In theory concubinage has always been condemned by the Catholic Church; in practice the local clergy has done little to enforce this disapproval and in fact counsels patience and resignation on the part of wives. . . .

The *querida* is a prestige item, like a Cadillac. Men flaunt their mistresses, take other men to call on them, provide them with luxuries usually far more expensive than those they give their wives. Panamanians boast, "We do not hide our mistresses like the Costa Ricans." *Queridas* are the subject of gossip at the market and in the park; everyone seems to know all about such relationships and to tolerate them. It is generally agreed that a man has a right to as many mistresses as he can afford.

— Reading No. 20 —

THE CUBAN STEW[21]

Fernando Ortiz, the grand old man of Cuban letters, whose intellectual and artistic interests have been very broad during his long and productive life, has devoted some of his best pages to a consideration of what is closest to his heart—the people of Cuba.

✓   ✓   ✓

Cubanidad does not consist simply in having been born on Cuban soil, nor does it have anything to do with the political citizenship which everyone born on Cuban soil enjoys . . . or suffers, as the case may be. Cubanidad is more than a meter of earth moistened by the first

[21] Fernando Ortiz. "Los factores humanos de la cubanidad," *Revista Bimestre Cubana*, XLV (La Habana, 1940), pp. 165-169, *passim*. Reprinted by permission.

tears of a new-born infant, more than a few square inches
of white paper marked with seal and signature symbolic
of official recognition of a legal relationship, true or
fictitious. Nor is cubanidad transmitted at the time of
conception; there is no Cuban race. . . . Cubanidad is
principally the peculiar quality of a culture, the Cuban
culture. In modern jargon, cubanidad is a matter of spiritual condition, a complex of sentiments, ideas and attitudes. . . .

It has often been said that Cuba is a crucible of human elements. . . . But perhaps one could find another
metaphor more precise, more comprehensive and more
appropriate to a Cuban audience. . . . We would do
well to choose a Cuban simile, a metaphorical Cubanism,
for we would make ourselves better understood, sooner
and in greater detail. Cuba is an *ajiaco*.

And what is an ajiaco? It is the most typical and complex of stews, made from a variety of vegetables, "viands"
in our Cuban idiom, and from chunks of different kinds
of meat; all boiled together with water until the juice
is thick and succulent, and then seasoned with our typical
Cuban chile, the *ají* from which we derive the name of
the dish. . . .

The image of our creole ajiaco symbolizes for us the
formation of the Cuban nation. Let us follow the metaphor. First of all, the pot is open. This is Cuba, the island, the pot placed to boil on the fire of the tropics. . . .
Our ajiaco has a unique pot, our Cuban land, made of
clay and very open. Then, fire with a high flame and a
slow fire to simmer, dividing the cooking process in two;
this happens in Cuba, the unending fire of the sun but
with the rhythm of the seasons, wet and dry, heat hot
and temperate. Into the pot go substances of the greatest
variety of types and origins. The Indians gave us the
corn, the potato, the *malanga*, the yam and yucca, and
the ají which seasons the stew and the cassava bread with
which the good creoles of Camagüey and Oriente adorn
it before serving. This was the first ajiaco, the pre-Columbian ajiaco, with the flesh of rats, iguanas, crocodiles,
snakes, turtles, snails and other small game and seafood
unsavory to our modern palate. The Spanish threw out
these Indian meats and added their own. They brought,
along with their squashes and turnips their fresh beef,

jerked beef, dried beef, and *lacón*. All this gave a new savor to the Cuban ajiaco. With the European whites arrived the African blacks and these contributed the guinea hen, the banana, the *ñame,* and their cooking technique. Then came the Asians with their mysterious spices and the French with their educated palates to temper the causticity of savage pepper; and the Anglo-Americans with their domestic machinery which simplified the cooking and who wanted us to use their standard metal skillet in exchange for the earthen pot which nature gave us, along with the tropical heat to keep it warm, the water of the skies for the broth and the water of the seas to fill the salt cellar with crystals. All these have contributed to our national ajiaco.

By its very name the ajiaco is a linguistic ajiaco: from the plant, the Indo-Cuban *solanacea,* with a Negro-African linguistic root and a Castilian suffix to give the word its slightly despective overtones, employed very properly by a conqueror in referring to a colonial stew. And so the Cuban ajiaco has gone on boiling and simmering, on the open fire or on the back of the stove, clean and dirty, various as the ages which brought new human substances to be thrust into the pot by the hand of the chef, who, in this metaphor, is the ever-changing tide of history. In every era our nation has had, like the ajiaco, new, raw elements just thrown into the pot; a heterogeneous conglomeration of diverse races and cultures, of many meats and foodstuffs, which were stirred, mixed together, and disintegrated in the boiling of society; and down at the bottom of the stew there now rests a new mass, produced by the elements which upon disintegrating in this historic boiling have contributed their most durable essences to settle in a rich and tastily seasoned mixture, which has the true character of a new creation. A mixture of cuisines, of races, and of cultures. A thick broth of civilization which bubbles on the Caribbean fire.

— Reading No. 21 —

CUBAN LAND TENURE PROBLEMS[22]

Cuban land problems have some special aspects pe-
culiar to the island, but many of the basic obstacles to a
healthy agricultural development mentioned here are to
be found throughout Latin America.

↗   ↗   ↗

Agrarian reform has been a pillar in the political plat-
forms of nearly all aspiring Cuban leaders. During various
periods in the island's history, attempts toward redistribution of land, diversification of agriculture and less island dependence on world markets, have achieved only
partial success. The complexity and enormity of land
tenure problems permeate nearly every phase of Cuba's
economic and social life. During the rise of the modern
sugar industry the concentration of landholdings, through
a system of speculative, monopolistic land-ownership, was
made possible by the feudal system of distributing property in the colonial era during Spanish rule. Many of the
current problems of land taxation, vast size of properties
and little land available for thousands of migrant wage-
laborers, are traceable to the period when Cuba exported
solely to Spain. . . .

The utter confusion resulting from the breakdown of
the Spanish land system encouraged land monopoly by
the wealthy, and aided unscrupulous landholders to increase their estates through property frauds. Since accurate location of granted lands was nearly impossible,
it was exceedingly difficult to differentiate granted lands
from state property. As a result, vast acreage in many

[22] Robert B. Batchelder, "The Evolution of Cuban Land Tenure
and Its Relation to Certain Agro-Economic Problems,"
The Southwestern Social Science Quarterly, XXXII
(1952-1953), pp. 239-246, *passim*. Reprinted by permission.

of the island's provinces passed into private ownership without due process by law. . . .

The Industrial Revolution in Europe and the United States profoundly altered the colonial sugar industry in Cuba. The influx of new technical skills and capital from abroad heralded the death of the old sugar mill in Cuba, which was an agro-industrial entity with its grinding capacity balanced with local supply. The rapid construction of the modern *central*, or mill, required more land devoted to sugar in order that production would meet greater plant capacity. Thus, the old system of communal lands underwent change because clear title of ownership was necessary if new mills were to obtain control of greater acreages. During the period of United States occupation, the American Military Government appointed a commission of Cuban lawyers to analyze existing problems of land tenure. Out of the findings of this commission came General Wood's order providing for division of communal estates by special court process. The successful establishment of private property for communal landownership laid the foundation for the corporate development of vast private estates or *latifundios*. . . .

Land hoarding in Cuba was encouraged by the absence of a rural real estate tax commensurate with the productive value of the soil. Currently, the burden of revenue is derived from taxes on basic consumer items and urban real estate. Actually, the present Cuban system of land taxation is but a slightly amended relic of the late 1880's. . . .

Land reform necessarily will be slow owing to the complexity of land tenure problems. Redistribution of land is only one phase of a comprehensive program needed to create a highly productive and balanced agricultural economy. Capital must be made available to farmers at low rates of interest; markets cooperatively organized; better agricultural methods taught the people, and many other forms of socio-economic aid should be advanced. In the past 15 years, considerable progress has been achieved in diversification of agriculture. . . .

Adjacent to urban agglomerations, many holdings are devoted to crops needed to sustain city dwellers. In various parts of the island off-season specialty crops are grown, which enter the northern markets of the United

States. . . . Notable progress also has been made in reducing the dominance of sugar and sugar-products in the island's list of exports. Products other than sugar, tobacco and cattle, which are traditional exports, account for nearly 20 per cent of the value of commodities sent abroad today. . . .

The wealth of Cuba mainly lies in her tropical location and vast acreages of fertile land. Through technical improvements in crop production and careful planning, Cuba is attempting to reach a solution in which the plantation system—the mainstay of Cuba's economy—will be maintained at peak efficiency, while at the same time, the complex land tenure problems be resolved so that the majority of the people will receive directly a larger share of the island's wealth.

— Reading No. 22 —

HAITIAN PROBLEMS[23]

Since the government has always been a dictatorship, limited or absolute, subject to no party control, the incumbents of office have never had the experience of being constantly reminded by their opponents of the misery of daily wants of the population. After a hundred years the people have learned that relief is not to be expected from politicians. . . . To most governments of the past century Haiti's problem has been only one: to frustrate insurrection. There is evidence that recent administrations have busied themselves with the country's internal problems, although none of them has been adequately solved. . . . The problems remain . . . the three outstanding are overpopulation, with all its accompanying ills, health, and education. . . .

[23] James G. Leyburn, *The Haitian People,* New Haven: Yale University Press, 1941, pp. 3-13, 265-289, *passim.* Reprinted by permission.

Probably the most striking phenomenon in the country is its division into two social groups. So rigidly are the class lines set that *caste* is the only word to describe the effective separation of aristocrats from the masses. The caste system is a vivid fact, for it regulates a person's profession, speech, religion, marriage, family life, politics, clothes, social mobility—in short, his whole life from cradle to grave . . . even the most casual observer is aware that Haiti cannot by any stretch of the imagination be called a democratic country, with an open class system. The two castes are the élite and the masses. They are as different as day from night, as nobleman from peasant; and they are as separate as oil and water. The élite are generally reckoned to compose at the outside not more than three per cent of the population.

The élite do not work with their hands. This is the cardinal rule of Haitian society. . . . All the professions, most governmental and military offices, and the large business enterprises are effectively closed to young men of the masses. . . . The peasant woman, from childhood onward, is an indefatigable laborer, absolutely indispensable to the economic life of the country. . . . The aristocratic woman . . . is rarely active in business. . . . Her place is definitely in the home. The second infallible test of membership in the élite caste is education and an ability to speak French. . . . The élite live in towns. . . . Formal marriage is another requisite for membership in the élite. . . . Religion affords another distinction between high and low. Haiti has a folk religion . . . called Vodun . . . African in origin, Créole in its language, and homely in its creed and practice. Few members of the élite, however their hearts may yearn for the consoling security of Vodun, dare openly to acknowledge their "atavism" or participate in the cult. They must be Catholics or agnostics . . . because Vodun is a *folk* religion. . . . The final and most complicated distinction between the two castes is skin color . . . the lighter the skin, the more likely a person is to belong to the élite. . . .

The peasant is conservative. . . . Progress and improvement are to him only vague abstractions, much less real than the struggle for mere existence. . . .

To associate for any length of time with the upper
classes of Haitian society is to be aware of a deep unrest. . . . What worries the élite? . . . the élite man
knows that he is a cultured gentleman in the truest sense.
For years he has seen tourist ships landing hundreds of
Americans each week at Port-au-Prince and Cap-Haitian;
he has seen the mad revelry of some of these whites, their
ill-mannered vulgarity, their superficiality of mind, their
poor taste. He knows well enough that it is not fair to
judge a whole nation by a few representatives, yet it is
clear to him that these raucous whites regard themselves,
and are by others regarded, as lords of creation who need
never worry about social acceptance. The Haitian knows
himself the superior of most of these white people,
whether the test be intellectual or on the basis of gentility.
Nevertheless, the white inferior is preferred by all the
world to his Haitian superior. The white American can
go anywhere and, with his carefree self-assurance, see all
doors open to him; the cultured Haitian can go few places
from home, and in even those few many doors are yet
closed in his face. . . .

Thoughtful people know well enough that it is possible
to improve the lot of the people. But if the peasant should
be well educated he would become ambitious; where then
would be the monopoly which is now held by the aristocrats on wealth, government, education? Merest self-inter-
est prompts one to defend the status quo. This definitely
worries many of the upper group. Aware that so long as
conditions remain as they are Haiti will be poor and
backward, they are nevertheless not ready to promote
what would be a thorough-going social revolution. If any
government should become oversolicitous for the well-
being of the masses, it would soon find itself bitterly opposed by the upper class. In the long run, what will be
the result of keeping things as they are? Élite who know
their history can find several possible answers, no one of
which appeals to them: a peasants' revolt, a Reign of
Terror, intervention by a foreign power. They are on the
horns of a dilemma: if as rulers they promote material
welfare, they lose their present positions of security; if
they do not promote a change, violent change will unseat
them.

"NOT A MAN, A NATIONAL SYMBOL: GENERALISSIMO RAFAEL LEÓNIDAS TRUJILLO"[24]

The date on which Trujillo began his rule in the Dominican Republic, August 16, 1930, is each year commemorated by the controlled press there. Trujillo's public relations representatives are active elsewhere, too. The issue of Auge, *from which this quotation comes, shows the Generalissimo receiving decorations and distinctions from the United States, Mexico, and the Vatican.*

✔   ✔   ✔

A nation born from the heart of one man: this could well be the title of the epic progress achieved in the last two and one-half decades in the Dominican Republic. . . . Twenty-five years ago, Generalissimo Doctor Rafael Leónidas Trujillo Molina took charge of the government. . . . He has become a symbol.

Under this symbol, under this protective and beneficial force, every enterprise in Dominican life is undertaken. Because of him, life and property are respected with exemplary zeal; under this symbol, every work can be undertaken in peace, and laws can be applied with inexorable equity; this symbol represents security today and faith in the future. He is the guiding force which wisely has been able to steer safely the Ship of State from the dangerous seas which have threatened to sink it. And now, that it peacefully sails through calm waters, the grateful people call him "Chief," "Benefactor," and "Father."

[24] *Auge* (August 16, 1955, Mexico City), International Edition. No. 57, p. 9.

— Reading No. 24 —

PUERTO RICO'S CONTRIBUTIONS TO DEMOCRACY[25]

Luis Muñoz Marín, the first elected Governor of Puerto Rico and one of the ablest statesmen in the hemisphere, here presents his estimate of the meaning of the Commonwealth of Puerto Rico.

I believe that basically the democracy of Puerto Rico has contributed to the democracy of the Western Hemisphere a new form of political party, to which I have the honor to belong, the Popular Democratic Party. I say that this is a new form of political party because it has brought about, and is still carrying on, a peaceful revolution in Puerto Rico by completely legal processes. It is doing this, not by propounding doctrines, but by facing with open heart and open mind the great problems that for so many years have burdened my Puerto Rican compatriots in their daily lives. This is a revolution that is progressing without hide-bound, doctrinaire attitudes, and to my mind this is a contribution of considerable value to democracy. . . .

One method which we have finally developed in order to keep the political parties free of the influence of money is a law which provides that all political parties shall receive from public funds the legitimate expenses which a party must incur in its work in a democracy; these funds are provided in equal amounts to all political parties. To the party of which I have the honor to be the leader, which received 64 per cent of the votes in the last election, exactly the same amount is contributed for its ex-

[25] Address given by Governor Luis Muñoz Marín before the Inter-American Press Association, October 16, 1957. Mimeographed, pp. 1-4, *passim*. Reprinted by permission.

penses as is given to the smallest party, which obtained only 12 or 14 per cent of the votes at the last election. This frees the political parties from any ties or obligations of any kind to the economic interests that normally have to provide the campaign funds for political parties, and I believe that this is another important contribution that Puerto Rico has made to democracy.

Still another contribution which Puerto Rico is making to democracy is the creation of a new form of political association in a federal system of government. Since the first steps were taken and this new form of association established, Puerto Rico's relationship with the United States has been based on a pact which was approved both by the Congress and the President of the United States and by the electorate of Puerto Rico by direct ballot. Under this pact Puerto Rico is associated with the United States within a federal system of government on a basis of common citizenship, a common market, common currency, common defense, and common international political relation. In the field of culture Puerto Rico maintains relations with other countries but in its political relations it is part of the federal union. This system, under which all of the internal government of Puerto Rico is vested in the people of Puerto Rico, according to the constitution that was written and approved by that same people, is a creation that leaves the way open for new political forms.

Puerto Rico and its people are not working toward— and I should like my Latin American friends to understand this thoroughly, since at times it is a little difficult for them to grasp the matter because of the different historical traditions that exist in other parts of Latin America —Puerto Rico, I repeat, is not working toward independence; the Commonwealth is not an expedient that is to lead to independence. Neither is Puerto Rico going to become a federated state of the Union; the Commonwealth is not a way station along the road to that political status. It is a political creation, constitutional in itself. It is new, but it is not doomed to remain static; it can develop, it can grow, but it is my opinion and apparently the opinion of most Puerto Ricans that it will have to grow of its own nature toward independence and not toward statehood. I want to tell you, my friends, that if

the people of Puerto Rico were to find that the alterna-
tive to independence was colonialism, then they would
dauntlessly face all the economic dangers of independence, because there is no colonialist spirit among them.
What they have done is to create a new form of freedom
that suits their own special needs, economic as well as
cultural. And that is why we feel proud to be the creators
of the plan for a commonwealth in voluntary association
with the United States of America. But please note that
it is a form of freedom; if it were not, we would not be
in favor of it.

— Reading No. 25 —

THE COLOMBIAN UPPER CLASS: WHITE, PRIVILEGED, COMPETENT[26]

The gaps between the classes in Colombia are so great
and so rigid that in a time of social ferment violence is
always potentially present. Even when social and economic resentments merely simmer below the surface, the
stream of national life may give a deceptive appearance
of placidity that belies the facts and misleads the observer.

To a very great extent, this is due to the frames of
reference created by the upper classes themselves. Colombian upperclass people take their place in society by right
of birth. The Great Families are still names to conjure
with, and connections with them by marriage, bloodlines,
or financial and social ties are both desirable and a kind

[26] Vernon Lee Fluharty, *Dance of the Millions,* Pittsburgh:
University of Pittsburgh Press, 1957, pp. 182-187, *passim.*
Reprinted by permission.

of *Paz y Salvo* (safe-conduct card) to most areas of preference and privilege.

Due to the centuries-old tradition of caste, those born into the upper classes inherit the unshakable assumption that the lower classes are by nature inferior—they are those who cook, serve, clean, run errands, bow and scrape, and perform the hard and the menial tasks of the society. . . .

There is, then, considerable justification for the maintenance of control monopoly by the upper crust of Colombia's social layer cake. But that is not to justify, nor to indicate that the monopoly should be continued indefinitely. The real question, however, arises from the long tradition of the monopoly: how to break it without doing harm to the whole society; how to admit the masses to fuller participation as they impatiently demand a voice in directions.

This dilemma must be resolved in terms of the willingness of the upper class to share power, a willingness so far not demonstrated. Status in society in Colombia has always been determined by birth and by ownership of land. . . .

But to say that the upper classes of Colombia are an élite percentage of the population is not to say enough. Basically, the white Colombian is a Spaniard, with a complex racial heritage and he is therefore, a complex personality. Charming and witty, he is skeptical often to the point of cynicism, capable of extreme violence and frequent cruelty. . . .

Theories and disputations over abstractions charm him unutterably. But he is also extremely clear-headed and practical in everyday affairs. This upper-class Colombian has made his mistakes, but he has also done a first-class job of building the national economy and the national culture into a respectable edifice worthy of admiration. In brief, he is quite a fellow. His one blind spot is that he has always felt that the economy was for *him;* that culture (not necessarily esthetics) was for his sole consumption. . . .

As a young man, this upper-class Colombian was probably educated in a Colombian prep school or university, and later went to the United States or Europe for further study. Very likely he plays polo, or did before easy living made the game too strenuous for both him and the horse. Still, he keeps up an interest in sports, gambles with moderation, holds large quantities of whiskey (Scotch preferred) well, and loves a good story, either from himself or others.

Quite often he is highly literate, having gone through a youthful period of writing doggerel, although now he prefers the stock reports to Valencia or Mistral. Rather earlier than North Americans, he learned about women, and he will maintain an active, practicing interest in them long after he has married the daughter of his father's best friend who, like himself, is of the élite. His interest in politics may take him to Congress or to a cabinet post, or to service on the directorate of his party, even while he heads his own company or runs his coffee business or hovers over his investments. Books and ideas will be a part of his life, running always a little ahead of practical matters. . . .

All summaries are oversimplification, and this one does not tell all of the upper classes in Colombia. Perhaps it rather understates the case for the oligarchy: the culture, the industry, the tenaciousness, the vision in certain regards, the true gentility, the many-sided comprehension which marks these upperclass people. But it can never, on the other hand, overstate the case of the mental rigidity of the upper-class social outlook, a rigidity which prevents the development of a truly national outlook for all Colombians.

For this same high-caste Colombian has tended, and still tends, to worship at the shrine of social immobility through the vertical stratum; to perpetuate a set of values which excludes the great mass of people from participation in the national life; and in this regard, he is both arbitrary and short-sighted.

— Reading No. 26 —

COLOMBIAN INDIVIDUALISM[27]

Why have governments in Colombia found it so diffi-cult to create a sense of national unity? Here Jorge Padilla, a Colombian writer, gives his answer.

Our aptitude for anarchism is incredible. We are churl-ishly individualistic. No great movement has ever taken place here because there are as many opinions as people. In 1946, when Liberalism split over Turbay and Gaitán, the Turbay Directorate sent a telegraphic circular around with the rules for the campaign. One day it received from a hamlet lost in the depths of the provinces a message, in reply, which said:

> Liberal Directorate, Bogotá
>   Have received circular. Respectfully advise am only Liberal in this town. And *I* am divided. Regards.
>   Pedro Pirateque

We are an archipelago of opinions, of theses, of con-trary interests. The greatest difficulty for a governor is, therefore, that of knowing exactly where our uncoercible, our unstable, our paradoxical public opinion flows. Every Colombian is a political party.

[27]As quoted by Vernon L. Fluharty, *Dance of the Millions,* Pittsburgh: University of Pittsburgh Press, 1957, pp. 167-168. Reprinted by permission.

— Reading No. 27 —

THE PACT OF SITGES, JULY 20, 1957[28]

Two Colombian ex-Presidents, the Conservative Laureano Gómez and the Liberal Alberto Lleras Camargo, drew up in the Spanish seaport Sitges a notable and unique agreement which aimed at bringing political peace to their nation by proposing a bipartisan government for a period of twelve years.

We Colombians must have above all a policy of peace, or rather, a policy which will bring peace. It is absolutely essential that a political order be brought about in which each individual may know his rights, his obligations, and the penalties which all must pay who violate those rights and those obligations. All parties agree that order can be created only on the basis of the constitutional precepts which were violated. To put the entire Constitution into effect is the first of our duties. From the harmonious functioning of a government controlled by its various separate branches acting as brakes peace will be born, and it is useless to seek peace until there exists a juridical order respected by all. . . .

Elections . . . should be preceded by arrangements which would permit the maintenance of a government or a series of governments based on an ample coalition of the parties, which would continue until institutions backed up by the unequivocal support of the citizenry have enough strength so that civic dispute can be carried on without fear of *coups d'état*. . . .

Congress, with its two chambers as provided for in the Constitution, should be reestablished in the first election. But it appears to be necessary that this election should

[28] El Tiempo (Bogotá, July 30, 1957).

have a limit which only the people can impose, if they so desire: namely, that neither of the two parties may have a majority within the legislative body, thus avoiding that Congress be distracted from its formidable task of rebuilding a shattered nation. . . . Also, in order to avoid that the control of either chamber should fall into the hands of one of its members, it must be established that Congressional decisions be taken by a qualified majority superior in number to one more than half of its members. . . .

Once [having] extinguished the passions and cured the wounds which the struggle for power and dominion by the violent factions within our parties has caused in the present generation, it will be possible to return without fear to a fully democratic system of civilized and open contest for the predominance of the ideas of each party; but never, certainly, to the criterion of the totalitarian hegemony of one party over the other which has been the efficient cause of our recent and tremendous disasters.

A legislative body organized in this manner, immune to sectarianism, should be balanced by an executive branch of party cooperation and coalition in which the now omnipotent power of the President in the selection and dismissal of government functionaries would be limited. The first limit must be the urgently needed creation of a career of civil service which will go a long way toward suppressing the idea that to the political victor belong the spoils of the vanquished and the right to change the public administration from top to bottom, substituting his new favorites for the experienced employees. This has been the tragedy of each change of government in Colombia, not because of the importance (non-existent) of the bureaucrats in comparison with the rest of the nation's population, but because the employees and aspirants for government employment are those who promote violence in order to defend their jobs or who loose violence in order to obtain a government position. To this insignificant and, with few exceptions, inept minority the nation owes many of its troubles and one may anticipate that there the latent threat of another outbreak of violence is to be found, if the decision is not made, once and for all, to provide a constitutional guarantee for administrative work and to make of these function-

aries once and for all citizens neutral in the political
struggle, to create, in short, a respectable and serious career for specialists in the management of public business,
whose duties shall not be changed by political changes
and whose character shall not be debased by doctrinal
submission to each change of situation.

The other limit would be that the President of the
Republic, upon choosing his co-laborers in the cabinet,
should be obliged to maintain the political proportion
which the parties will have within the legislative chambers. . . .

From what has been said it is clear that what has been
proposed to the consideration of the parties has no other
goal than that of achieving peace for Colombia and of
creating a permanent foundation for peace, making peace
the first objective of the two traditional sectors of republican opinion. . . . So long as peace does not exist,
so long as there is organized or sporadic violence, so long
as there are those who profit from murdering or threaten-
ing their fellow citizens, so long as there are those who
have made a regular career of a warlike and savage mode
of life, the remaining problems of Colombia will find no
solution, not even the economic problems, which are extremely sensitive to uncertainty and insecurity. . . .

For this task there is one indispensable condition: the
liberty of the press. If it should suffer the slightest diminution or inhibition, the fulfillment of a just program for
the constitutional and moral restoration of the fatherland
would be made impossible. . . . The greatest obligation
and the great responsibility of the parties is to defend
with all their energy the liberty of the press. For this
purpose a bipartisan commission should be constituted
at the highest level to guard the full exercise of this
recently achieved liberty. This commission should be
strongly supported by public writers so that it will be
practicable for it to make use of the necessary measures
of protection when some violation of the freedom of the
press is attempted. . . .

LABOR LAWS IN VENEZUELA[29]

Under Venezuelan law the petroleum and mining companies are subject to special requirements in addition to those affecting standard labor-management relations. The following list of requirements indicates the scope of the labor law as it applies to such companies (many of the provisions cited below, however, apply to all employers):

1. 75 per cent of the work force must consist of Venezuelan nationals . . . ;

2. If the place of non-extractive employment in the oil and mining business is more than two kilometers (one and a quarter miles) from the center of the residential area in which the workers reside, the companies must pay for or provide transportation to and from work;

3. If a worker is discharged for reasons other than dishonesty, damaging property, unjustified absence from work for three or more days during the preceding month, and so forth, the employer is required to pay the worker one-half month's wages for each year (or fraction thereof exceeding eight months) of employment;

4. The worker in question is also entitled to unemployment aid at the rate of five days' wages if he has worked from three to six months and up to fifteen days' wages for each year of work for the employer; the worker is entitled to receive such payments even if he moves immediately to another job;

5. Paid vacations are to be granted the worker at the rate of fifteen working days for each year of work.

6. The worker is entitled to share in profits to the extent of at least 10 per cent, up to a limit of two months' wages (oil company workers receive the equivalent of two months' wages at Christmas time almost every year);

[29] Virgil Salera, "Some Problems of the Venezuelan Petroleum Industry," *Inter-American Economic Affairs,* IX (Summer, 1955), No. 1, pp. 79-81. Reprinted by permission.

7. In the computation of profit-sharing liabilities to the workers, the company may not offset past losses against the current year's profits;

8. Pregnant women are entitled to "sufficient indemnity" (regarded as the equivalent of regular wages) for the period of six weeks prior to and six weeks after childbirth;

9. Oil and mining companies must: a. Build workers' "camps" in order to provide housing with at least 4½ square meters of surface per inhabitant; b. Rent living quarters at not more than one-third of 1 per cent of the value of the property per month. That is, the rental must not exceed 4 per cent on the current value of the investment in workers' houses. Actually, the usual practice is to charge substantially less than permitted by law, or only a token rental—one that does not even cover depreciation; c. Provide the community with drinking water, lighting and sanitary facilities; d. Provide primary schools; e. Provide hospitals; f. Provide quarters for the union, at a rental based on the same formula that applies in the case of workers' housing; g. Provide technical schools in which the workers may pursue studies relative to their trade; h. Provide one advanced scholarship annually for the children of workers when the company's labor force consists of 400 to 2,000 workers, and three such scholarships when more than 2,000 workers are employed; i. In the event of accidental death, the company must make a payment equal to two years' wages to relatives of the deceased.

10. Overtime and holiday pay is at the rate of 125 per cent of the daily hourly wage for each hour of overtime or holiday work.[30]

[30] Based on the *Ley del Trabajo,* Caracas, 1952.

ADULATION OF DICTATORS IN VENEZUELA[31]

Venezuela has suffered dictatorship longer than most Latin American countries, and she has also produced some of the most penetrating and biting studies of the phenomenon of dictatorship.

✓   ✓   ✓

In order to get along in Venezuela, it is not sufficient for well-meaning men to make an honest living from their work, secluding themselves in their homes and thus isolating themselves from the surrounding corruption. Something still more difficult, almost impossible for certain men, is required: it is necessary to stay in the good graces of the government, to pamper the governors, to fulfill at all times the rites of adulation imposed by the professional flatterers: it is necessary to call the potbellied politician an Apollo, the moron a genius, the hippopotamus a hippogriff, the robber a man of honor, the assassin generous, the Torquemada a liberal. And that is not enough: the favorites and subalterns also have their vanities and require their measure of praise. . . .

It is an established fact that whoever does not flatter the magistrates and their favorites is no friend of the government; and it is an established policy that whoever is not a friend of the government goes to jail. On any day of the month, the saint's day of any swine who may be occupying the presidency of any state, or a position in any ministry, or the governorship of the federal district, some policeman is likely to sally forth to collect signatures to felicitate the President, Minister, or Governor, and to note down in another list the names of those who refuse

[31] Pedro María Morante, *Los felicitadores,* Caracas: Tipografía Garrido, 1952, pp. 7-11, *passim.* Reprinted by permission.

to participate in this Asiatic salaam. Would anyone prefer not to sign, thus assuring his appearance on the list of those who on the next morning will wake up in jail, accused enemies of the government? Why make this useless sacrifice, which will not be imitated, but ridiculed? . . .

An opportune felicitation not only has the negative value of avoiding a visit to jail; it also has a positive value —it helps one to obtain a good job: . . . : Merit is valueless: to spend a lifetime in order to become an expert in some science; to burn the midnight oil studying law; to master medical science or mathematical knowledge, all these are less effective than knowing how to flatter. Those who, knowing their own worth, are so proud as not to prostrate themselves, discover that all the roads which lead to success are thronged with incompetents on the way to arriving under official protection. And the incompetents who have already arrived on top establish a reign of ineptitude over ability, the predomination of cleverness over probity, and loose to the air their noisy braying concert, believing themselves as harmonious as an orchestra of birds. The humiliating triumph of mediocrity! . . .

To improve the national soul, the governors ought to reward rather than punish the independent individuals. General Gómez would make a great contribution if he would order the Secretary General to publish this notice:

"The President of the Republic is not to be felicitated."

— Reading No. 30 —

"SOWING THE OIL" IN VENEZUELA[32]

The López Contreras government recognized that the nation was basically backward, that what it needed was a long-range program of modernizing and diversifying its means of production, a vast improvement in its communication system, and a bettering of the health and educational standards of its people. Such a program required capital. It could come from but one source—oil. *"Sembrar el petroleo"* was the slogan adopted. The idea was to take the money obtained by the extraction of wealth from Venezuela's soil and sow it into the land in order to grow a healthy diversified economy which when ripened would provide for all its own needs and be independent of petroleum.

To agriculture went the government's primary attention, a separate ministry being established in 1936. Subsidies were extended . . . to a number of farm products, and crop-expansion and livestock improvement programs were launched. . . .

To build public works, the government accepted construction projects from the petroleum companies in lieu of taxes. . . . Shell built a road from Mene Grande to Motatán, thus connecting the Andrés with the Maracaibo Basin; Standard put up a hospital in Maracaibo and constructed several roads in Monagas; and both Shell and Standard erected public works in Anzoátegui. . . .

On no point is the record so black as on the question of the government's investment of its huge petroleum revenues. Though tremendous tax wealth has come in, the program of "sowing the petroleum" has accomplished

[32] Edwin Lieuwen, *Petroleum in Venezuela, A History*, Berkeley and Los Angeles: University of California Press, 1954, pp. 83-84, 119-120. Reprinted by permission.

surprisingly little. The mass of the people in Venezuela today are poor, unhealthy, illiterate, and live in the most primitive surroundings. The economy is still shockingly backward.

. . . The tremendous petroleum revenues have, on the whole, not been used intelligently. Too much goes to the army and the huge government bureaucracy. . . . The amount of funds peculated by dishonest officials has been tremendous.

The state becomes more and more opulent; the populace continues to live in misery. Meanwhile the nation becomes more and more dependent on a single extractive industry, more and more sensitive to events abroad. There is much to the argument that the industry is so powerful that the state can do little to stop its absorbing force, but this does not excuse the government for its failure to invest its funds wisely in a long-range program of economic and social improvement.

The rulers of Venezuela have been the army officers of Táchira. They made, and are still making, policy. They must bear the responsibility for it.

— Reading No. 31 —

VENEZUELA CAN ACHIEVE A STABLE, CIVILIZED GOVERNMENT[33]

Rómulo Betancourt, long-time leader of the Acción Democrática Party, wrote a notable polemic, from which this extract is taken, on the past and future of his country

[33] Rómulo Betancourt, *Venezuela: Política y petróleo*, Mexico City: Fondo de Cultura Económica, 1956, pp. 768-770, 774. Reprinted by permission.

while he was living in exile. Now, as President (1958-), he has an opportunity to put his ideas into practice.

✓   ✓   ✓

One might suppose that the possibility of reestablishing and stabilizing a civilized systems of government in Venezuela is remote indeed. The uninterrupted flow of petroleum, with the financial returns which come from this export, and the international complicities which have been an effective support for dictatorial regimes in our country, seem to guarantee a rosy future for dictatorship in Venezuela. This conclusion is the result of a hasty analysis. In Venezuela the collective will to recover lost liberties, encouraged and channeled by the political forces organized by the parties, has not died out. And history proves that in any country where there are numerous groups within the population—the best armed intellectually and morally, in the long run—which persevere in their resistance to institutionalized arbitrariness, these groups always succeed eventually in imposing democratic norms of government and administration.

This is what Andrés Eloy Blanco said, in the well chosen words of a great poet and intuitive politician, in the lecture which was his last will and testament, given a few hours before he died, before the members of *Acción Democrática* in exile in Mexico: "It is necessary to acknowledge the importance of the economic realities, but we must also remember the reality of our people. They are as a people backward economically and resplendent in their epic struggle; underdeveloped by any economic criterion and millionaires in human wealth; small in number but great in their heroism. Among the people emotional values and above all the human factor are vital. Our prime material and our greatest wealth is our human wealth."

But other tendencies, which also go toward putting an optimistic face on the political future of Venezuela, should be noted. Some of these are related to the national reality itself; others result from recent historical events, universal in scale, which have occurred within the American scene.

Regarding Venezuela, it is coming to be realized that the regime imposed upon the nation without its consent is a historical anachronism, which goes against the degree

of development already achieved by the country . . .
Its daring disdain of all norms of good government are as
contrary to the needs of a highly evolved society as its
police methods of dealing with the citizenry are repugnant
to the entire population. The fact is that Venezuela is no
longer what she was in the days of Castro and of Gómez,
when she had scarcely two million inhabitants and was a
backward, bucolic nation, without industries, isolated
from the world in an era of difficult communications, and
with a population scourged by yellow fever and lack of
culture. Today we form part of a modern nation, a nation
which has passed through the industrial revolution of the
twentieth century, with a national territory largely made
safe from tropical diseases, and with a population which
exceeds five million, of whom half a million are workers
living in industrial and extractive centers. Large segments
of this population are cultured and there is a numerous,
well informed middle class. The nation is no longer a
walled island but, on the contrary, due to its geographic
location and its economic potential, it is a plexis of aereal
and maritime inter-communications. The radio has nulli-
fied the attempts of the governors to isolate us from the
world as Paraguay was isolated in the nineteenth century
under Francia. Thus one can understand why the determining majority of Venezuelans . . . is against a
regime which makes every effort to continue to apply the
tribal methods of Cipriano Castro and Juan Vicente
Gómez to an adult nation in the process of accelerated
growth. . . .

And if the Venezuelan nation is different today from
what it was in the times of Gómez, today's army is also
distinct from the mountaineers of that era, a primitive
horde commanded by ignorant cut-throats. The requirements of national growth itself and the technological complexity of modern arms have forced the rise of groups of
officials possessing appreciable personal culture in some
branches of the armed forces, especially the Navy and the
Air Force. It was groups from among these cultivated
sectors of the armed forces who have contributed to the
changes overcoming anti-democratic situations in some
Latin American countries. . . .

Our reasoned and profound conviction is that it will be
possible to create a stable form of government in our

country which will respect popular liberties, and among them the fundamental right of suffrage; a government concerned to resolve by modern and rational means the problems of the collectivity; a government honorable in its handling of public monies and disposed to convince foreign investors that their capital may enter the nation for the purpose of legal business, and not to despoil our natural resources and trample upon the rights of the Venezuelan worker. In short, a government capable of orienting and conducting the national democratic revolution that is at the present moment a historical necessity for Venezuela, and which can no longer be postponed.

— Reading No. 32 —

THE NATURE OF MEXICAN CULTURE[34]

As a background for the analysis of the experience of Mexican students in the United States, a rapid review is given of the nature of the culture of the urban middle and upper class, from which most of the Mexican students come.

✔   ✔   ✔

All observers and students tend to emphasize the heterogeneity of Mexican culture, both in terms of class and of region. . . . Regional, class, and rural-urban differences still characterize Mexico. In addition Mexico has also undergone a major social revolution in the past forty years and any attempt to define themes, values, or attitudes must reckon with a time dimension that may

[34] Ralph L. Beals and Norman D. Humphrey, *No Frontier to Learning. The Mexican Student in the United States,* Minneapolis: University of Minnesota Press, 1957, pp. 9-27, *passim.* Reprinted by permission.

introduce enormous contradictions. As in thirty years Mexico has moved from pack train to motor truck and airplane, so Mexican society has moved from a feudal society toward an industrial society. The traditional elite has been destroyed, impoverished, or relegated to positions of little power or influence. . . .

Political leadership and governmental participation are marked by a group of professional politicians and the influence of a growing bureaucracy. Intellectuals participate to a greater extent and wield much more influence than in the United States. Despite the dominance of a one-party system, effective political democracy is growing. The expanding middle class is increasingly represented. Low salaries are reflected in the *mordida* (system of bribery). . . .

There is extensive participation, both organized and informal, by business, industry, agriculture, and labor in the formation of government economic policy. . . . The military is an important political force, but in Mexico its role and power have been reduced. Increasingly the viewpoint of the army is dominated by progressive, middleclass aspirations. . . .

Most Mexicans are professed Catholics, but in rural areas much of the religious participation is of a folk character. Particularly in urban centers many Mexicans are indifferent toward religion, or, although still considering themselves devout Catholics, are strongly anti-clerical. Secularism pervades most aspects of urban society, particularly among the middle and upper classes and the military.

Separation of church and state is far more complete than in most Latin American countries, and efforts to limit the economic privileges and political power of the Catholic Church have occurred several times in Mexican history. . . . Church organizations are now legally denied corporate status and hence may not own property; monastic foundations and religious schools are prohibited; public religious processions and the wearing of clerical garb on the streets are illegal; and the clergy must be citizens. Enforcement of these laws, never complete, in recent years has become more lax. . . .

The family remains the basic social and economic unit of Mexico. . . . Sons often remain economically dependent or involved in family enterprises. Not infrequently sons continue to live at home until middle age or until their children are too numerous to be accommodated in the ancestral home. . . . Social functions within the home tend to include only relatives. Nepotism in government and business is common and expected . . . but in some urban settlings there is some diminution of the patriarchal character of the family, coupled with rising social position for women. . . .

Possibly nowhere in the Latin-Catholic world has the godparent relationship been so elaborated as in Mexico. Not only does the child treat his godparents like true parents, but parents and godparents (*compadres*) treat each other like, and are often closer than, true siblings. . . . The *compadrazco* influence reaches into the highest levels of business and government. For example, the decision to extend the federal rural school system into an area may be determined by the fact that a local political leader is a *compadre* of the minister of education. . . .

The revolution . . . has destroyed the political position, much of the economic power, and to some degree the social prestige of the traditional elite. The self-made man can rise high in Mexico today and a marked degree of mobility has replaced the relatively static pre-revolutionary society. . . .

Along with the social and economic changes of the revolution have come changes in value orientations. Among the old elite and in rural areas traditional values tend to persist. Wealth itself is not a symbol of success, but is sought for personal security and, often, in rural areas, to carry out the ritual obligations of the folk religion. . . .

These values, insofar as they persist in the urban areas, possibly find their expression through investment in urban real estate, contributing to the overdevelopment of office and apartment property. But increasingly in urban Mexico, status differences are measured in terms of the pecuniary calculus. Everywhere one finds a grasping for money, the "fast buck" philosophy, the quick speculative big-return venture rather than the sound and long-run modest-profit enterprise, and a low level of business morality. The symbols of monetary success are the swarms of Cadillacs, the fabulous houses of such sections as Chapultepec

Heights and San Angel, the private *fronton* courts (for ball games) corresponding to the Hollywood swimming pools, elaborate dress, and lavish public entertainment of friends in restaurants. . . .

Some of the leading themes and value orientations found among urban upper class and in some parts of the middle class [are]: First loyalty is owed to the family. . . . Men are superior to women and require a freer sex life. The father is the authoritarian head of the household. He has exceptional powers of discipline. While the wife is cloistered, the husband may have mistresses or a series of promiscuous relationships without real danger of divorce. . . . The mother is the center of the home. She forms strong ties with her sons, to whom she looks for moral sustenance and economic support if widowed. Mexican motion pictures abound in tear-jerking sentimentality about relations between mother and son. . . . Women are both weak and passionate and hence without aid they are unable to protect their virtue. "Good" women, therefore, must be sequestered and supervised. . . .

Race consciousness is primarily found in the traditional elite which denies and looks down upon any Indian mixture. . . . *La raza* is the source of spiritual unity. . . . The concept . . . has little to do with race; rather it is an idealization and glorification of Latin culture as opposed to Anglo-Saxon culture. . . . To lead the good life one must have non-material goods. . . . Time, work, and money do not have value in themselves. Certain kinds of work are degrading (for example, most work with the hands). . . . Spiritual and intellectual matters are more important than material. Honor hence may be given the scholar, even though he is poor and without family. . . . The wealthy and status-conscious intellectual who cannot carry a package on the street may perform prodigies of literary production. Mexican (and European) cultures are spiritual; Anglo-Saxons (especially North Americans) are materialistic. . . .

Ritual is to be valued. . . . Death is to be accepted, or death is present in life. . . . In both prehistoric and modern Mexico the death motif is common. . . . Tavera mentions the "morbid eagerness" of Mexican medical students in dissection and discusses the precise details published in newspapers of traffic fatalities, the elaboration of funeral rites, and the elaborate celebration of the Day of the Dead. . . . The popularity of bullfighting is associated with this attitude. . . .

Life is to be lived dramatically. Mexicans love action, movement, color, and sound. The haggling of the market place, the extravagant audience behavior at the bull fight, the love of adventure and daring, the wealth of flowers from palace to hovel, are all expressions of this set of values . . . nearly every foreign commentator emphasizes the noisiness of Mexico. . . . The abuses of the sound truck, the loud-speaker, and the radio suggest that Mexico's traditional love of music is partly love of noise.

Music is the true expression of Mexico. Mexicans are deeply, emotionally responsive to Mexican music; even sophisticates who profess to scorn the shoddiness of much contemporary popular music succumb to the authentic folk music. A recent attempt to bar strolling musicians from overcrowded busses in Mexico City aroused a storm of public indignation. . . .

The emergent values of Mexico are less clearly defined. . . . There is, however, a decided movement toward the urban-industrial values widely held in western Europe and North American cultures. The following items are merely suggestive [as emergent values]. *Mexico must become an integrated nation.* . . . An important new theme related to nationalism is *indigenismo,* a product of the revolution. It consists of identification with, and to some extent glorification of, the Indian, particularly the Indian past. It is no accident that Mexico spends a larger proportion of its national revenue on archaeological research than perhaps any other country in the world. . . . Related to, but to some extent in opposition to extreme forms of *indigenismo,* is the movement to "incorporate the Indian into national life," one of the revolutionary slogans. So long as the Indian masses do not participate effectively in the national life, they are seen as an obstacle to the development of a national culture and a modern state. Despite verbal commitments on an abstract level, in concrete situations most students do in fact look down upon the Indian. . . .

Mexico must participate independently in international affairs. Mexicans chafe under the knowledge that a foreign policy completely independent of the United States is impossible. At the same time they aspire toward leadership of the Spanish-American countries. As Mexico now is or will soon become the largest Spanish-speaking country in the world in population as it already is in area, strivings, for independence and international leadership will be intensified.

Education is the hope of Mexico. Mass education as an instrument of progress has become a positive value for at least a sizeable minority of all classes. This is a marked departure from earlier advocacy of a classical education for the elite only. . . .

Industrialization and social change are desirable. Determination to "build a steel and concrete civilization" is accompanied by the belief that this will solve Mexico's problems and by a rejection of the belief in a static society. . . .

Art is a part of life. Contemporary art is in part a product of the revolutionary period. Artists tend to be political minded, mural art is for the masses, and Mexican thought and feeling are communicated through artistic work on public buildings. . . .

Mexican culture is in transition, but the direction of its movement is not yet uniform. . . .

— Reading No. 33 —

THE MEXICAN FIESTA[35]

One of the wisest interpretations of Mexico comes from the pen of the poet Octavio Paz in his series of brilliant essays El laberinto de la soledad (*Mexico City: Ediciones*

[35] Octavio Paz, "Todos Santos, Día de Muertos," *Evergreen Review,* No. 7 (New York, 1959), pp. 22-27, *passim.* Reprinted by permission.

Cuadernos Americanos, 1950). Here is a selection from the third chapter.

✦   ✦   ✦

The solitary Mexican loves fiestas and public gatherings. Any occasion for getting together will serve, any pretext to stop the flow of time and commemorate men and events with festivals and ceremonies. We are a ritual people, and this characteristic enriches both our imaginations and our sensibilities, which are equally sharp and alert. The art of the fiestas has been debased almost everywhere else, but not in Mexico. There are few places in the world where it is possible to take part in a spectacle like our great religious fiestas with their violent primary colors, their bizarre costumes and dances, their fireworks and ceremonies, and their inexhaustible welter of surprises: the fruit, candy, toys and other objects sold on these days in the plazas and open-air markets.

Our calendar is crowded with fiestas. There are certain days when the whole country, from the most remote villages to the largest cities, prays, shouts, feasts, gets drunk and kills, in honor of the Virgin of Guadalupe or Benito Juárez. . . .

But the fiestas which the Church and State provide for the country as a whole are not enough. The life of every city and village is ruled by a patron saint whose blessing is celebrated with devout regularity. Neighborhoods and trades also have their annual fiestas, their ceremonies and fairs. And each one of us—atheist, Catholic, or merely indifferent—has his own saint's day, which he observes every year. . . .

. . . How could a poor Mexican live without the two or three annual fiestas that make up for his poverty and misery? Fiestas are our only luxury. They replace, and are perhaps better than, the theater and vacations, Anglo-Saxon weekends and cocktail parties, the bourgeois reception, the Mediterranean café.

In all of these ceremonies—national or local, trade or family—the Mexican opens out. They all give him a chance to reveal himself and to converse with God, country, friends or relations. During these days the silent Mexican whistles, shouts, sings, shoots off fireworks, discharges his pistol into the air. He discharges his soul. And his shout, like the rockets we love so much, ascends to the heavens, explodes into green, red, blue and white lights, and falls dizzily to earth with a trail of golden sparks. This is the night when friends who have not exchanged more than the prescribed courtesies for months get drunk together, trade confidences, weep over the same troubles, discover that they are brothers, and sometimes, to prove it, kill each other. The night is full of songs and loud cries. . . . Now and then, it is true, the happiness ends badly, in quarrels, insults, pistol shots, stabbings. But these too are part of the fiesta, for the Mexican does not seek amusement: he seeks to escape from himself, to leap over the wall of solitude that confines him during the rest of the year. All are possessed by violence and frenzy. Their souls explode like the colors and voices and emotions. Do they forget themselves and show their true faces? Nobody knows. The important thing is to go out, open a way, get drunk on noise, people, colors. Mexico is celebrating a fiesta. And this fiesta, shot through with lightning and delirium, is the brilliant reverse to our silence and apathy, our reticence and gloom. . . .

Thanks to the fiesta the Mexican opens out, participates, communes with his fellows and with the values that give meaning to his religious or political existence. And it is significant that a country as sorrowful as ours should have so many and such joyous fiestas. Their frequency, their brilliance and excitement, the enthusiasm with which we take part, all suggest that without them we would explode. They free us, if only momentarily, from the thwarted impulses, the inflammable desires that we carry within us. . . .

Our fiestas are explosions. Life and death, joy and sorrow, music and mere noise are united, not to recreate or recognize themselves, but to swallow each other up. There is nothing so joyous as a Mexican fiesta, but there is also nothing so sorrowful. Fiesta night is also a night of mourning.

ART AND POLITICS IN MEXICO[36]

The colorful and powerful murals which were painted during the Mexican Revolution were political documents as well as artistic creations. Diego Rivera symbolized the artist-politician type of these years; José Clemente Orozco viewed such a mixture with suspicion and irony.

One of the themes which has most preoccupied Mexican muralists has been the history of Mexico. Some have enlisted themselves among one of the factions of historians and others have been independent thinkers, but all have become experts and commentators of great force and penetration. It is really wonderful. The discrepancy evident in the paintings is the reflection of the anarchy and confusion of historical studies, the cause or effect of the fact that our personality is not yet well defined in our consciousness, although it is of course perfectly defined in the field of action. We do not yet know who we are, like a nation suffering from amnesia. We are continuously classifying ourselves as Indians, creoles, or *mestizos,* thinking only of the mixture of bloods, as though we were dealing with race horses, and from this system of classification parties have arisen saturated with hatred, which are engaged in a life struggle, the indigenists and the Hispanists. . . .

The whole history of Mexico seems to be written exclusively from the point of view of race. Apparently the problem is to proclaim or force the opponent to accept the superiority of one of the two races, and the worst of it is that this is no domestic quarrel, for foreign pens have taken part and are taking part in the writing of our

[36] José Clemente Orozco, *Autobiografía,* Mexico: Ediciones Occidente, 1945, pp. 99-106, *passim.* Reprinted by permission.

history, often for questionable purposes. The work of our historians seems like a boxing match between Indianists and Hispanists, with a foreigner for referee.

The theory that Mexico is necessarily Indian, Spanish, or mestizo is a false basis for the definition of our personality. The Spanish race is not one, but many and diverse. Spain was formed by Iberians, Celts, Romans, Greeks, Phoenicians, Jews, Arabs, Goths, Berbers, and Gypsies and each one of these groups was itself mixed. What is the race of the Spaniards and the Portuguese who have come to the Americas in the last four centuries?

In modern times other races have entered into the populations of Spain, Portugal and Hispanic America, one might say all the races of the world, and in considerable number. Nor does it appear that the American indigenes were of a single race, to judge by the diversity of type, custom, language, and degree of culture to which they had attained before contact with Europe.

The consequences of this emphasis upon the racial theory to the exclusion of all others are very grave. The antagonism between the races is stimulated. The conquest of Mexico by Hernando Cortés and his hosts seems to have taken place only yesterday. It is more alive today than the outrages of Pancho Villa. It seems that the assault on the great Teocalli and the Noche Triste and the destruction of Tenochtitlán could not have taken place four centuries ago, but rather last year, or even yesterday. . . . This antagonism is fatal because all the races are extremely proud. Not one will admit defeat or final submission. . . .

To achieve unity, peace and progress it might suffice to do away forever with the question of race; never again to talk of Indians, Spaniards and mestizos; to relegate the whole business of the conquest to purely speculative studies and to leave it where it belongs, in the sixteenth century; to treat the Indian, not as an "Indian," but as a man, equal to any other man, as we would treat a Basque or a Spaniard from Andalucia. If we must have a Department of Indian Affairs, why not a Department of Mestizo or Creole Affairs, too? These Indian Affairs remind one of a Department of Poor Devils, Department of Unfortunates Not Yet of Age who will never be able to do anything for themselves and require people of other races to think for them and provide them graciously with whatever they need. . . . A Department of the Licentious or of the Sick would be less humiliating. The indigenous race should be nothing other than one of many who have gone to make up the Hispanic race, of the same category and with the same rights as all the others. . . .

But this lovely ideal would be ruined by the indigenists. In their opinion the conquest was not as it ought to have been. Instead of sending cruel, ambitious captains, Spain should have sent a numerous delegation of ethnologists, anthropologists, archeologists, civil engineers, dental surgeons, veterinarians, doctors, rural school teachers, agronomists, Red Cross nurses, philosophers, philologists, biologists, art critics, muralists, and learnéd historians. Upon arriving in Veracruz allegorical carts decorated with flowers would debark from the caravels, and in one of them Cortés and his captains, each carrying a little basket of Easter lilies, a great quantity of flowers, confetti and streamers for use along the road to Tlaxcala and the great Tenochtitlán; and then to pay homage to the powerful Moctezuma, to establish bacteriological, urological, x-ray and ultra-violet ray laboratories, a Department of Public Assistance, universities, kindergartens, libraries and savings and loan associations. The Spaniards, instead of accepting the frequent gifts of Aztec and Toltec maidens, should have brought handsome girls from Andalucia and Galicia to be offered to Moctezuma and Cuauhtemoc. Alvarado, Ordaz, Sandoval and the other heroes of the conquest should have been assigned the task of guarding the cities in ruins so that nothing would be lost of the tremendous pre-Columbian art. The Spaniards should have learned the seven hundred eighty-two different languages then in use here; respected the indigenous religion and left Huitzilopochtli in his place; given free hand-outs of seeds, agricultural machinery and livestock; constructed houses and given them to the peasants; organized the *ejidos* and cooperatives; built highways and bridges; taught new industries and sports, all in a nice way, gently and with affection; encouraged human sacrifice and founded a great packing house for human meat with a fattening division and modern machinery for refrigeration and canning; suggested most respectfully to Moctezuma the possibility of establishing democracy, but without taking any of their privileges away from the aristocracy, in order to please everybody.

— Reading No. 35 —

THE CACTUS CURTAIN: CONFORMITY IN MEXICAN ART[37]

A young painter, José Luis Cuevas, here illustrates the essential vigor of Mexican art by repudiating the official view.

✓   ✓   ✓

I do not pretend to be a leader of the young, and I am not trying to recruit an army of rebels to storm the Palace of Fine Arts. I will limit myself to stating what I firmly believe to be the convictions of other members of my generation both in the fine arts and in other intellectual fields. . . .

Juan is a fictional character, but he is based on the actual people who swarm around our national culture. They stifle and terrify it, while those who ought to fight back are too apathetic or too frightened to speak up. . . .

Juan was fifteen years old. His father was a plumber, or a cobbler, or perhaps a minor official, one of those who, for a ten peso bribe, will settle within the legal period what would otherwise take months.

Juan was born with a talent that occurs very often among the population of the Republic of Mexico. This

[37] Cuevas, "The Cactus Curtain. An Open Letter on Conformity in Mexican Art," *Evergreen Review,* No. 7 (New York, 1959), pp. 111-120, *passim.* Reprinted by permission. Footnotes 38-40 appear in the article.

talent, this rich and ancient legacy, was not that of taking bribes, an infection poisoning the blood of the whole country, but of creating another, unknown world, the world of art.

Juan stood out in grade-school because of his excellent drawings. A school inspector saw them and told his teacher to encourage him. This continued until one day, Juan was given a prize and entered art school. . . .

They had taught Juan at La Esmeralda to draw simplified figures—smooth, undulant, curvilinear, with large hands and feet—and to use special effects such as foreshortening, so that certain intellectuals would say that he produced "strong" works of profound popular origin. They were not two-dimensional works. They tried to achieve three-dimensionality by an almost automatic method of drawing, a strict, uniform intensity of line. With such a formula, all is solved: it works equally well for portraying a man with a bandanna, an Indian woman selling flowers in the market, a worker in the oil fields, or one of those proletarian mother-and-child scenes which have been turned out for over thirty years without there having intervened, for the good of Mexican art, a single Malthusian or neo-Malthusian to hinder such an empty repetition of maternity.

Juan had not had access to books on the art of other countries either in school or in the public library, much less in the Palace of Fine Arts. Nor were there any museums in which he could see foreign art of the present or the past. When there was an exhibit of some artist who was not Mexican or who refused to follow the style he had been taught to believe was the only one, Juan's friends told him it was not worth seeing, because it pertained to an exhausted, degenerate culture, to inferior races that have nothing like the grandeur and purity of the Mexican race, which is the only one in the world that has complete command of the truth. . . .

But one day in a bookstore on the Alameda Juan saw an art magazine containing things very different from his own work. Some of them were unintelligible to him, and others struck him as absurd, but all of them fascinated him. "So there are artists in other countries too," he said to himself, "not just here in Mexico."

. . . He joined a national association, where both his

errors and good judgment would be protected as long as
he followed the line traced previously by who knows what
comrade. There were conquests to be realized both in
the salon and the association, and new demands to be
made: "Give us more walls to decorate for the people!"
Juan's two friends told him that this was the newest and
clearest demand of the courageous young men who paint
in Mexico, but he had read in a history of Mexican painting that it had been the hue and cry for almost forty
years. However, it was convenient for him to follow the
majority. Perhaps he would receive a fat commission.
When the others shook their clenched fists, he did too. . . .

I have not wanted to become a Juan; on the contrary,
I have fought against the Juans all my life. Against
vulgarity and mediocrity. Against superficiality and conformity. Against the standardized opinions that are
parroted over and over again, without interruption, from
the opening of an exhibit to the discussion afterwards at
the café. I protest against this crude, limited, provincial,
nationalistic Mexico of the Juans, but thus far I have
been answered only with personal attacks, even though my
own attacks have always been aimed at works of art and
the theories behind them, never at personalities. . . .

I should also admit that the Mexico I have attacked is
not the only one. There is another Mexico, one that I
deeply respect and admire: the Mexico of Orozco, Alfonso
Reyes, Silvestre Revueltas, Antonio Caso, Carlos Chávez,
Goitia, Tamayo, Octavio Paz, Octavio Barreda, Carlos
Pellicer, Manuel Bravo, Nacho López.[38] I am proud there
is a publishing project in Mexico like the Fondo de Cultura
Económica, and a rostrum like *México en la Cultura*[39] for
the expression of nonconformist opinions. I am delighted
when I hear praise for *Los Olvidados* and *Raíces*[40] in

---

[38] The late Orozco was a famous painter, as are Goitia and
    Tamayo. Alfonso Reyes, Antonio Caso, Octavio Paz,
    Octavio Barreda and Carlos Pellicer are writers. The
    late Silvestre Revueltas was a composer, as is Carlos
    Chávez. Manuel Alvarez Bravo and Nacho López are
    photographers.
[39] *México en la Cultura* is the weekly cultural supplement of
    the daily *Novedades*.
[40] *Los Olvidados* was shown as *The Young and the Damned*,
    and *Raíces* as *The Roots*.

other countries, although both films were box-office failures at home. It is this other Mexico that encourages me to protest, because it is the true, universal Mexico, open to the whole world without losing its own essential characteristics.

There is a younger generation in Mexico with ideals similar to those I have been discussing. I wish to associate myself with it. I am not setting myself up as an arbiter, and I am not seeking disciples. I approve of many different tendencies and directions, of many roads in art . . . but only when they are free and meaningful extensions of life itself. What I want in my country's art are broad highways leading out to the rest of the world, rather than narrow trails connecting one adobe village with another.

FURTHER READING

GENERAL

History has had such an impressive share in shaping modern Latin America that the student will wish to keep a well-written survey, such as Hubert Herring's *A History of Latin America From the Beginning to the Present* (Alfred A. Knopf, 1955), close at hand, or the briefer *The Evolution of Modern Latin America* (Oxford University Press, 1946), by Robin A. Humphreys. For a general and imaginative approach, see *This New World: The Civilization of Latin America* (E. P. Dutton & Co., 1954), by William L. Schurz.

Geography continues to be a powerful influence, too, and Preston E. James' *Latin America* (Odyssey Press, 3rd ed., 1959) is a standard guide with excellent maps.

On economic development, W. S. Woytinski has given a brief, informative, and refreshingly balanced treatment in *The U.S. and Latin America's Economy* (Tamiment Institute, New York [1958]). *Literary Currents in Hispanic America* (Harvard University Press, 1945), by Pedro Henríquez Ureña is focused on literature but has much to say on intellectual development generally.

On particular topics, Robert J. Alexander has compiled *Communism in Latin America* (Rutgers University Press, 1957) on that widely discussed topic. John J. Johnson's *Political Change in Latin America* (Stanford University Press, 1948) is a pioneering examination of the growth in political power of the middle classes. Kingsley Davis edited a challenging symposium "A Crowding Hemisphere: Population Change in the Hemisphere," *Annals of the American Academy of Political and Social Science,* vol. 316 (Philadelphia, March,

1958). For views of the exciting public buildings and private residences recently constructed, see Henry Russell Hitchcock, *Latin American Architecture Since 1945* (Museum of Modern Art, New York, 1955). A recent compact and sensible view on U.S. policy problems is Thomas W. Palmer, Jr., *Search for a Latin American Policy* (University of Florida Press, 1957). For an informed, optimistic view on religious affairs, see John T. Considine, *New Horizons in Latin America* (New York, 1958).

The literature pouring from the presses inside and outside of Latin America is enormous in quantity, but spotty in quality. For authoritative guides consult R. A. Humphreys, *Latin American History—A Guide to the Literature in English* (Oxford University Press, 1958), the annual *Handbook of Latin American Studies* (University of Florida Press) edited at the Hispanic Foundation of the Library of Congress, and the quarterly *Hispanic American Historical Review* (Duke University Press). Most of the books listed below have valuable bibliographies.

Among the reviews the quarterly *Inter-American Economic Affairs* (Washington, D.C.) edited by Simon Hanson is much the most lively and controversial. *The Americas* is a handsome popular monthly isued in English, Portuguese, and Spanish editions by the Organization of American States (Washington, D.C.). The Foreign Policy Association (New York) issues competently prepared reports on current topics, the American Geographical Society (New York) has an attractive series of brief reports on individual countries or regions in its *Focus* series, and the Pan American Union (Washington, D.C.) has a wide variety of factual brochures on countries, products, cities, etc., at reasonable prices. The Library of Congress, the National Archives, and other libraries and government agencies (Commerce, Agriculture, Mines, etc.) in Washington, D.C., constitute the greatest center in the world on the past and present of Latin America. The Economic Commission for Latin America of the United Nations has a series of up-to-date studies of value.

Press coverage in American newspapers varies greatly. *The New York Times* provides more information than any other paper, while the *Christian Science Monitor* has regularly interpretative articles of unusual value. *The Chicago Tribune, The Cleveland Plain Dealer,* and *The St. Louis Post-Despatch* are among the other newspapers giving special attention to Latin America. Ronald Hilton at Stanford University edits a monthly *Hispanic American Report* which gives the only detailed coverage (c. 700 pages annually) of current affairs in Latin America, based on a wide variety of press clippings and some other sources. A substantial index to Volumes I-VII, covering issues for 1946-1952 of the *Report,* was published in 1957. An unfortunate example of the decline of U.S. interest in Latin America after World War II was the disappearance of the annual survey volume *Inter-American Affairs* (Columbia University Press, 1942-1946), edited by Arthur P. Whitaker with the assistance of a number of specialists.

Volumes scheduled for publication in late 1959 by the Council on Foreign Relations in New York are a collaborative work *Social Change in Latin America* and Edwin Lieuwen's *Army and Politics in Latin America*.

CENTRAL AMERICA

ADAMS, RICHARD N., *Cultural Survey of Panama—Nicaragua —Guatemala—El Salvador—Honduras,* Washington, D.C.: Pan American Sanitary Bureau, 1957. A 699 page mass of valuable, unindexed information on Panama and all the Central American republics except Costa Rica, whose Director General of Public Health refused to allow the survey to be carried on.

BIESANZ, JOHN and MAVIS, *Costa Rican Life,* New York: Columbia University Press, 1944.

————, *The People of Panama,* New York: Columbia University Press, 1955. Sociological studies by a man-and-wife team. The volume on Panama is more lively and stimulating, and the Costa Rican monograph more statistical.

EALY, LAWRENCE O., *The Republic of Panama in World Affairs, 1903-1950,* Philadelphia: University of Pennsylvania Press, 1951.

INTERNATIONAL BANK FOR RECONSTRUCTION AND DEVELOPMENT, *The Economic Development of Nicaragua,* Baltimore: Johns Hopkins Press, 1953.

JONES, CHESTER LLOYD, *Costa Rica and Civilization in the Caribbean,* 2nd ed., San José, Costa Rica: Editorial Borrasé Hermanos, 1941. Though now somewhat out of date statistically and principally devoted to Costa Rica, this volume was so carefully prepared that it still has value.

————, *Guatemala, Past and Present,* Minneapolis: University of Minnesota Press, 1940. Written twenty years ago, this volume still remains one of the few basic books on a Central American country.

LOOMIS, CHARLES P., and others, eds., *Turrialba. Social Systems and the Introduction of Change,* Glencoe, Illinois: The Free Press, 1953. Pioneer study of a Costa Rican community in order to understand the problems and processes of culture change in an underdeveloped area.

MARTZ, JOHN D., *Central America. The Crisis and the Challenge,* Chapel Hill: University of North Carolina Press, 1959. The only up-to-date, though somewhat pessimistic, description of political and economic affairs in the post-World War II period. Also contains challenging interpretations of dictators and of United States policy.

MAY, STACY AND GALO PLAZA, *The United Fruit Company in Latin America,* Washington, D.C.: National Planning Association, 1958. Emphasizes economic aspects and gives slight attention to such controversial matters as the Company's treatment of competitors and involvement in Central American politics.

PIKE, FREDERICK B., "The Catholic Church in Central America," *The Review of Politics* XXI University of Notre Dame Press, January, 1959), No. 1, pp. 83-113. Historical review plus a realistic description of present-day conditions. Includes some information on Protestant activity.

SCHNEIDER, RONALD M., *Communism in Guatemala. 1944-1954,* New York: Praeger, 1958. Foreign Policy Research Institute Series, No. 7, University of Pennsylvania. Based on a mass of information.

SILVERT, K. H., *A Study in Government: Guatemala,* New Orleans: Middle American Research Institute, Tulane University, 1954, p. 239. The first half is concerned with the Revolution of 1944 and the structure of the national, departmental, and local governments. The text of the principal Guatemalan constitution is reproduced in the second part of this volume.

STOKES, WILLIAM S., *Honduras: An Area Study in Government,* Madison: University of Wisconsin Press, 1950. Solid study, with much information conveniently organized.

WALLICH, HENRY C. and JOHN H. ADLER, *Public Finance in a Developing Country. El Salvador—A Case Study,* Cambridge: Harvard University Press, 1951.

THE CARIBBEAN

ABRAHAMS, PETER, *Jamaica: An Island Mosaic,* London: Her Majesty's Stationery Office, 1957.

BLANSHARD, PAUL, *Democracy and Empire in the Caribbean,* New York: The Macmillan Co., 1947. Personal conclusions based on an extensive first-hand experience, 1942-1946, in Caribbean affairs as a U.S. official. Both provocative and informative, though now somewhat out of date.

The British Caribbean, London: Oxford University Press, 1957. "A brief political and economic survey," compiled by the Royal Institute of International Affairs.

Developments Towards Self-Government in the Caribbean, The Hague, 1955, Netherlands Universities Foundation for International Cooperation. A symposium covering British, Dutch, French, and U.S. territory, with selected bibliography.

HANSEN, M. and H. WELLS, eds., "Puerto Rico, A Study in Democratic Development," *The Annals of the American Academy of Political and Social Science,* Vol. 285 (1953), pp. 1-166.

INTERNATIONAL BANK FOR RECONSTRUCTION AND DEVELOPMENT, *Surinam: Recommendations for a Ten Year Development Program,* Baltimore: Johns Hopkins Press, 1952.

LEYBURN, JAMES G., *The Haitian People,* New Haven: Yale University Press, 1941. Still the best single volume.

MUÑOZ MARÍN, LUIS. "Puerto Rico and the U.S., Their Future Together," *Foreign Affairs* (July, 1954), pp. 541-551. An official statement by the present Governor.

NELSON, LOWRY, *Rural Cuba,* Minneapolis: University of Minnesota Press, 1950. A detailed study by an agricultural sociologist.

ORTIZ, FERNANDO, *Cuban Counterpoint: Tobacco and Sugar,* New York: Alfred A. Knopf, 1947. An informed and entertaining interpretation, by a leading Cuban writer.

PARRY, J. H. and P. M. SHERLOCK, *A Short History of the West Indies,* London: Macmillan & Co., Ltd., 1956. Valuable survey, emphasizing the British territories.

REVERT, EUGÈNE, *La France d'Amérique: Martinique, Guadeloupe, Guyane, Saint-Pierre et Miquelon,* Paris: Editions Maritimes et Coloniales, 1955.

RUBIN, VERA, ed., *Caribbean Studies: A Symposium,* Kingston, Jamaica: Institute of Social and Economic Research, University College of the West Indies, 1957. Specialized anthropological and sociological studies.

SWAN, MICHAEL, *British Guiana: The Land of Six Peoples,* London: Her Majesty's Stationery Office, 1957. Attractive and interesting general presentation, with much information.

WILGUS, A. CURTIS, ed., *The Caribbean,* Gainesville: University of Florida Press, 1951-1958, 8 vols. Since 1950 the University of Florida has held annually a conference on Caribbean affairs with participants from business, government, and the academic world, and has printed the proceedings. Much interesting information on a variety of matters, though necessarily uneven in quality. Issued with slightly different title each year.

COLOMBIA AND VENEZUELA

FLUHARTY, VERNON LEE, *Dance of the Millions. Military Rule and the Social Revolution in Colombia, 1930-1956.* Pittsburgh: University of Pittsburgh Press, 1957. A controversial interpretation, with much valuable information gained from extensive experiences and wide reading. The late Professor Fluharty's support of the dictator General Gustavo Rojas Pinilla has obscured somewhat the value of the other material he presents.

FALS-BORDO, ORLANDO, *Peasant Society in the Colombian Andes. A Sociological Study,* Gainesville: University of Florida Press, 1955. An important work, based on field research.

LIEUWEN, EDWIN, *Petroleum in Venezuela. A History,* Berkeley: University of California Press, 1954. Solid study.

MARSLAND, W. D. and A. L., *Venezuela Through its History,* New York: Thomas Y. Crowell Co., 1954. Attractively written story.

PARSONS, JAMES J., *Antioqueño Colonization in Western Columbia,* Berkeley: University of California Press, 1949. Ibero-Americana, 32. Careful analysis of the most important single region of Colombia.

ROMOLI, KATHLEEN, *Colombia. Gateway to South America,* New York: Doubleday, Doran, 1941. Now somewhat out of date, but an interesting popular introduction and for long one of the few good books in English on Colombia.

ROURKE, THOMAS (D. J. Clinton), *Gómez, Tyrant of the Andes,* New York: William Morrow & Co., 1936. An attack. For a defense, see Pedro M. Arcaya, *The Gómez Regime in Venezuela* (Washington, D.C.: privately printed, 1936).

WHITAKER, ARTHUR P., *The United States and South America.*

The Northern Republics, Cambridge: Harvard University Press, 1948. Includes Colombia, Venezuela, and the Andean countries. Useful comparisons and valuable bibliography.

WISE, GEORGE S. CAUDILLO, *A Portrait of Antonio Guzmán Blanco,* New York: Columbia University Press, 1951.

YBARRA, T. R., *Young Man in Caracas,* New York: Ives Washburn, 1941. Amusing autobiography.

MEXICO

BRENNER, ANITA and GEORGE R. LEIGHTON, *The Wind that Swept Mexico. The History of the Mexican Revolution, 1910-1942,* New York: Harper & Brothers, 1943. Remarkable photographs, with pithy captions.

CASO, ALFONSO, *The Aztecs. People of the Sun,* Norman: University of Oklahoma Press, 1958. Handsomely produced translation of a study by one of Mexico's leading scholars.

COVARRUBIAS, MIGUEL, *Mexico South: The Isthmus of Tehuantepec,* New York: Alfred A. Knopf, 1946. Well-illustrated socio-ethnological description.

CLINE, HOWARD F., "Mexican Community Studies," *Hispanic American Historical Review,* XXXII (Duke University Press, 1952), pp. 212-242. Bibliographical record and analysis of this prime material for the study of contemporary Mexico.

————, *The United States and Mexico,* Cambridge: Harvard University Press, 1953. Comprehensive treatment which goes far beyond its title. Excellent appendix of "Suggested Readings" (pp. 430-439).

"The Eye of Mexico," *Evergreen Review,* No. 7 (New York, 1959), pp. 22-213. Superb translations of such writers as Octavio Paz, Juan Rulfo, and Juan José Arreola.

GRUENING, ERNEST, *Mexico and Its Heritage,* New York: Century, 1928. A timeless volume on the background and development of the Revolution.

KNELLER, G. F., *The Education of the Mexican Nation,* New York: Columbia University Press, 1951. A general view by an able scholar.

[Mexican Issue] *The Texas Quarterly,* II (University of Texas Press: Spring, 1959), No. 1. The literature, art, philosophy, and other aspects of Mexican culture today. Handsomely produced, with many illustrations.

MORLEY, SYLVANUS, *The Ancient Maya,* 3rd ed., Stanford: Stanford University Press, 1956. Magnificently illustrated standard work.

MOSK, SANFORD A., *Industrial Revolution in Mexico,* Berkeley: University of California Press, 1954. Balanced, nontechnical account, now slightly out of date.

PARKES, HENRY BAMFORD, *A History of Mexico,* rev. ed., Boston: Houghton Mifflin Co., 1950. Still a useful work, though not a revaluation of Mexican history in the light of developments of the thirteen years since the first edition appeared.

POWELL, J. R., *The Mexican Petroleum Industry, 1938-1950,* Berkeley: University of California Press, 1956. Analysis of the problems and production of Petroleos Mexicanos, not a study of the expropriation.

ROMANELL, PATRICK, *Making of the Mexican Mind,* Lincoln: University of Nebraska Press, 1952. Sympathetic, provocative description of the intellectual scene.

SAUER, CARL O., "The Personality of Mexico," *Geographical Review,* XXXI (New York, 1941), pp. 353-364. Brilliant interpretation by a leading geographer.

SIMPSON, EYLER N., *The Ejido, Mexico's Way Out,* Chapel Hill: University of North Carolina Press, 1937. Fundamental work on land problems.

SIMPSON, LESLEY B., *Many Mexicos,* 3rd ed., Berkeley: University of California Press, 1952. Attractively written general account with thoughtful interpretation.

TANNENBAUM, FRANK, *Mexico: The Struggle for Peace and Bread,* New York: Alfred A. Knopf, 1951. A sober summary of what the Revolution has not accomplished.

TOOR, FRANCES, *A Treasury of Mexican Folkways,* New York: Crown Publishers, 1947. A rich collection, by an experienced folklorist long resident in Mexico.

TUCKER, WILLIAM P., *Government of Mexico Today,* Minneapolis: University of Minnesota Press, 1957. First comprehensive study in any language. A legalistic description, rather than analysis of the government in actual operation.

VAILLANT, GEORGE, *Aztecs of Mexico,* Garden City, N.Y.: Doubleday & Co., 1948. The standard work.

WHETTEN, NATHAN, *Rural Mexico,* Chicago: University of Chicago Press, 1948. A basic work, to be used with Eyler Simpson's *Ejido.*

INDEX

VAN NOSTRAND ANVIL BOOKS already published

1 *MAKING OF MODERN FRENCH MIND*—Kohn
2 *THE AMERICAN REVOLUTION*—Morris
3 *THE LATE VICTORIANS*—Ausubel
4 *WORLD IN THE 20th CENTURY*—Rev. Ed. Snyder
5 *50 DOCUMENTS OF THE 20th CENTURY*—Snyder
6 *THE AGE OF REASON*—Snyder
7 *MARX AND THE MARXISTS*—Hook
8 *NATIONALISM*—Kohn
9 *MODERN JAPAN*—Rev. Ed. Tiedemann
10 *50 DOCUMENTS OF THE 19th CENTURY*—Snyder
11 *CONSERVATISM*—Viereck
12 *THE PAPACY*—Corbett
13 *AGE OF THE REFORMATION*—Bainton
14 *DOCUMENTS IN AMERICAN HISTORY*—Morris
15 *CONTEMPORARY AFRICA*—Rev. Ed. Wallbank
16 *THE RUSSIAN REVOLUTIONS OF 1917*—Curtiss
17 *THE GREEK MIND*—Agard
18 *BRITISH CONSTITUTIONAL HISTORY SINCE 1832*—Schuyler and Weston
19 *THE NEGRO IN THE U.S.*—Logan
20 *AMERICAN CAPITALISM*—Hacker
21 *LIBERALISM*—Schapiro
22 *THE FRENCH REVOLUTION, 1789-1799*—Gershoy
23 *HISTORY OF MODERN GERMANY*—Snyder
24 *HISTORY OF MODERN RUSSIA*—Kohn
25 *NORTH ATLANTIC CIVILIZATION*—Kraus
26 *NATO*—Salvadori
27 *DOCUMENTS IN U.S. FOREIGN POLICY*—Brockway
28 *AMERICAN FARMERS' MOVEMENTS*—Shannon
29 *HISTORIC DECISIONS OF SUPREME COURT*—Swisher
30 *MEDIEVAL TOWN*—Mundy and Riesenberg
31 *REVOLUTION AND REACTION 1848-1852*—Bruun
32 *SOUTHEAST ASIA AND WORLD TODAY*—Buss
33 *HISTORIC DOCUMENTS OF W. W. I*—Snyder
34 *HISTORIC DOCUMENTS OF W. W. II*—Langsam
35 *ROMAN MIND AT WORK*—MacKendrick
36 *SHORT HISTORY OF CANADA*—Masters
37 *WESTWARD MOVEMENT IN U.S.*—Billington
38 *DOCUMENTS IN MEDIEVAL HISTORY*—Downs
39 *HISTORY OF AMERICAN BUSINESS*—Cochran
40 *DOCUMENTS IN CANADIAN HISTORY*—Talman
41 *FOUNDATIONS OF ISRAEL*—Janowsky
42 *MODERN CHINA*—Rowe
43 *BASIC HISTORY OF OLD SOUTH*—Stephenson
44 *THE BENELUX COUNTRIES*—Eyck
45 *MEXICO AND THE CARIBBEAN*—Hanke
46 *SOUTH AMERICA*—Hanke
47 *SOVIET FOREIGN POLICY, 1917-1941*—Kennan
48 *THE ERA OF REFORM, 1830-1860*—Commager
49 *EARLY CHRISTIANITY*—Bainton
50 *RISE AND FALL OF THE ROMANOVS*—Mazour
51 *CARDINAL DOCUMENTS IN BRITISH HISTORY*—Schuyler and Weston
52 *HABSBURG EMPIRE 1804-1918*—Kohn
53 *CAVOUR AND UNIFICATION OF ITALY*—Salvadori
54 *ERA OF CHARLEMAGNE*—Easton and Wieruszowski
55 *MAJOR DOCUMENTS IN AMERICAN ECONOMIC HISTORY, Vol. I*—Hacker
56 *MAJOR DOCUMENTS IN AMERICAN ECONOMIC HISTORY, Vol. II*—Hacker
57 *HISTORY OF THE CONFEDERACY*—Vandiver
58 *COLD WAR DIPLOMACY*—Graebner
59 *MOVEMENTS OF SOCIAL DISSENT IN MODERN EUROPE*—Schapiro
60 *MEDIEVAL COMMERCE*—Adelson
61 *THE PEOPLE'S REPUBLIC OF CHINA*—Buss
62 *WORLD COMMUNISM*—Hook
63 *ISLAM AND THE WEST*—Hitti